ROMAN ARCHITECTURE

Current and forthcoming titles in the Classical World Series

Classical World Series

ROMAN ARCHITECTURE

Martin Thorpe

Bristol Classical Press

General Editor: John H. Betts
Series Editor: Michael Gunningham

First published in 1995 by
Bristol Classical Press
an imprint of
Gerald Duckworth & Co. Ltd
48 Hoxton Square
London N1 6PB

A catalogue record for this book
is available from the British Library

ISBN 1-85399-421-9

Available in USA and Canada from:
Focus Information Group
PO Box 369
Newburyport
MA 01950

Printed in Great Britain by
The Cromwell Press Ltd., Melksham, Wiltshire

Contents

List of Illustrations

Acknowledgements

The following have kindly given permission for the reproduction of copyright material:

American School of Classical Studies, Athens, Agora Excavations: 4.1, from John M. Camp, *The Athenian Agora* (London, 1986).

Arnoldo Mondadori Editore, Milan: 5.1 from John Boardman, Jasper Griffin, Oswyn Murray (eds), *Oxford History of the Classical World* (Oxford, 1986).

Batsford Ltd: 1.2, 1.4, 1.5, 3.7, 3.9, 3.13, 4.11, 4.13, 4. 14, 5.3, A3, A4; from Frank Sear, *Roman Architecture* (London, 1982; 4.1, 4.2, 4.4, G.1. from Doreen Yarwood, *The Architecture of Europe* (London, 1974).

British Museum Press. 3.4, from T.W. Potter, *Roman Italy* (London, 1987); 4. 12, from Susan Woodford, *Cambridge Introduction to the History of Art: Greece & Rome* (Cambridge, 1982).

Building Centre Trust: 6.9, from *Real Architecture* (London, 1987)

P. Davies, D. Hemsoll & M. Wilson Jones: 1.7, from *Art History*, Vol. 10, No. 2.

Dover Publications Inc. G.2, G.4, from Vitruvius, *The Ten Books on Architecture*, tr. M.H. Morgan (New York, 1960).

FotoArchiv Büchner: 6.8

S. Gibson, J.S. Gregory, R. Ling & D. Murdoch (courtesy of the Pompeii Research Committee): 5.6

Ginn & Company: 5.7, from Peter Wyman, *Ostia*, (London, 1971).

Hodder & Stoughton: 6.4, from T.W. West, *A History of Architecture in Italy* (London, 1968)

Imperial Tobacco Ltd: 5.2, 5.4, from J.S. Ward-Perkins & Amanda Claridge, *Pompeii AD 79* (Bristol 1976)

National Gallery of Art, Washington DC: 1.3 – Panini, Interior of Pantheon (Samuel H. Kress Collection).

National Monuments Record, RCHME: 6.6

Penguin Books Ltd: 1.1. from William L. Macdonald, *The Pantheon: Design, Meaning & Progeny* (Harmondsworth, 1976); 6.5, from James S. Ackerman, Palladio (Harmondsworth, 1966)

Random House UK Ltd. 3.15, 4.8, from Iain Browning, *Jerash & the*

Decapolis (London, 1982); 3.6, from M.I. Finley (ed), *Atlas of Classical Archaeology* (London, 1977).

Society for Promotion of Roman Studies: 3.10, from J.B. Ward-Perkins, 'From Republic to Empire', *JRS LX* (London, 1970).

Sopritendenza per i beni culturali e ambientali, Aosta: 3.1, from *Archeologia in Valle d'Aosta* (Aosta, 1982).

Thames & Hudson Ltd: 3.5, from Mortimer Wheeler, *Roman Art & Architecture* (London, 1964); 6.3, 6.7, G.3, from John Summerson, *The Classical Language of Architecture* (London, 1980).

University of Alberta Press: 5.8, from Gustav Hermansen, *Ostia* (Edmonton, Alberta, 1982).

Yale University Press: A.5, from Axel Boethius, *Etruscan & Early Roman Architecture* (Harmondsworth, 1978); 6.1, from Richard Krautheimer, *Early Christian & Byzantine Architecture* (Harmondsworth, 1965); 3.8, 3.14, from William L. MacDonald, *The Architecture of the Roman Empire: Vol. II, An Urban Appraisal* (New Haven, 1986); 1.6, 2.2, 3.3, 3.11, 3.12, 3.13, 4.7, 4.10, 4.15, 5.5, 5.9, from J.B. Ward-Perkins, *Roman Imperial Architecture* (Harmondsworth, 1981).

We are grateful to the above and apologise for any inadvertent omissions. The following sources are also gratefully acknowledged:

The American Academy in Rome: 4.3, from Frank E. Brown, *Roman Architecture* (London, 1968).

Brockhampton Press: 4.6, from H. & R. Leacroft, *The Buildings of Ancient Rome* (Leicester, 1969).

The late Professor F. Castagnoli: 3.2.

Preface

Roman Architecture is a vast subject. It covers a period of at least eight hundred years and a geographical area from Spain to Syria and from Britain to North Africa; it ranges in scale from the planning of entire cities to the design of individual buildings; and it covers buildings of many kinds - religious and secular, public and domestic. In a brief, introductory book anything like full coverage is impossible. In addition, for many students, both in sixth forms and in universities, this will probably be their first approach to a topic from the visual arts. I have therefore tried to focus on a limited number of cities and buildings and to treat them at reasonable length rather than to hurry through a mere catalogue of names. The books listed in the Suggestions for Further Reading - many of them sumptuously illustrated - will help students who wish to explore the topic more widely or in greater detail.

It may be useful to point out here that the Glossary contains explanations for a number of architectural terms. Explanations of terms not listed there may occur in the main text and should be located by consulting the Index.

GCE Examination Boards are notoriously incapable of feeling, so I need not start my thanks by mentioning what was then the JMB for arousing my interest in Roman Architecture by setting it, under the rather snobbishly dismissive title 'Roman Building', as one of the topics in its A Level Classical Studies syllabus. To the students of Shrewsbury Sixth Form College, however – whose invariable good humour, high expectations, awkward questions, and (just occasionally) glazed expressions made them such a tantalising pleasure to teach – I should like to record my thanks for sustaining my interest in a topic I have come to find increasingly fascinating. I am grateful also to my wife, Meg, and my friends and colleagues, Irene Field and Alan Potter, who all read the book in draft. Their comments saved me from a number of blunders and greatly improved the clarity of expression, but they are not, of course, responsible for the faults of understanding or expression which remain.

Chapter 1

The Pantheon – 'Perfectest of all the Antiquities'

The Pantheon is the best preserved of all major Roman buildings, and this is probably why William Thomas described it as 'perfectest of all the antiquities' in his *History of Italy* (1549), but there are two further reasons for devoting the opening chapter to this one building. It illustrates many of the most important characteristics of Roman architecture, and its influence on later architects has been immense.

Appearance: (a) Forecourt, Facade and Porch

The main approach to the Pantheon lay through a formal gateway (fig. 1.1). Passing through this the visitor would find himself in a forecourt about 55-60m. wide and perhaps twice that in length, shut off from the world outside in an enclosed space open only to the sky. On either side of the gateway by which he had entered and down the two long sides there was a colonnade of grey granite columns. His view straight ahead towards the the temple was at first interrupted by a triumphal arch but as he moved forward and passed this, he could see ahead of him, framed by the side colonnades, a large but otherwise fairly conventional temple facade.

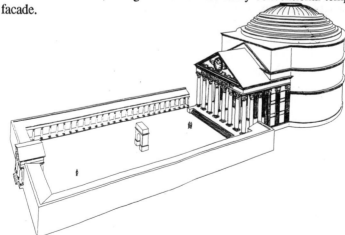

Fig. 1.1 Rome, Pantheon, forecourt

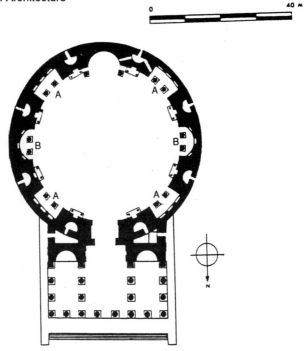

Fig. 1.2 Rome, Pantheon, plan

Eight huge Corinthian columns, over 14m. high, stretched across the forecourt, standing on a broad podium approached by a flight of five steps. Above them, the inscription in the entablature recorded the foundation of the temple and in the unusually steep pediment was carved an eagle with wings outstretched. Behind this facade, the porch was divided into three vaulted corridors (fig. 1.2) which ran back into deep shadow – the Pantheon faces almost due north. The columns of the porch were all unfluted monoliths, with capitals and bases of white marble. The shafts of the twelve outer columns were of grey and those of the four inner ones of red granite. The floor consisted of marble and granite slabs in a pattern of circles and rectangles.

The two side corridors ended in apses, perhaps containing statues, but as the visitor mounted the steps to enter the porch his eye would be caught by a dim light high up at the end of the centre corridor. Making his way through the darkness of the inner porch towards this light, he would find himself facing doors of bronze flanked by pilasters of white marble and would realise that the light came from a space beyond the doors, issuing into the porch through a bronze grille above them.

Pushing through the doors, he would enter that space.

Appearance: (b) Rotunda – Drum and Dome

He had emerged from a dark and rather confined space into one that was light and open, from one of straight lines and a clear sense of direction into one of curves, where it was difficult for the eye to find anywhere to rest. He stood in a large rotunda (fig. 1.3), made up of a circular drum and, resting on it, a hemispherical dome. The centre of the dome was open to the sky and a shaft of sunlight entering there illuminated the rich surface below. Wherever he looked, his eye was drawn on by the curved surfaces, up and across the dome or around the two cornices.

Fig. 1.3 Rome, Pantheon, interior (c. 1735)

The upper cornice swept round the top of the drum in an unbroken circle, while the lower one divided the inner surface of the drum into two bands. Immediately opposite the entrance doors, however, the lower cornice was interrupted by an apse which rose into the upper band. This established a longitudinal axis which helped the visitor find his bearing in the rotunda and appreciate its design.

The lower band of the drum did not present a uniform surface but an alternation of solid and broken wall, of projections and recesses, of light and shade. On either side, between entrance and apse, were three niches: the four on the diagonals (fig 1.2 A) were almost rectangular in plan, while those on the transverse axis (fig. 1.2 B) had curved rear walls. Across the front of the niches ran screens of pilasters and columns in coloured marbles – giallo antico (yellow/orange) for the diagonal ones, pavonazzetto (white with violet markings) for the transverse ones – which rose to the lower cornice and seemed to support the weight of the upper drum and dome above. Between these niches, the apse and the entrance, eight *aediculae* (miniature temple fronts) projected from the solid wall. Porphyry (a deep maroon stone) was used for the columns and entablatures of some of these, while the walls around them and in the niches were covered with panels of coloured marble including white, green and grey-green. There was a similar use of colour in the floor, which was paved in a pattern of alternating squares and circles of marbles, granites and porphyry.

The encircling wall of the upper band was more uniform. Fourteen blind windows were placed above the niches and *aediculae* of the lower band, but the bronze grilles which filled these helped to preserve an unbroken surface appearance. As in the band below, the appearance of the wall was enriched by a pattern of pilasters, panels and friezes in coloured marbles and other stones.

Above the cornice rose the dome. Its lower part was decorated with five rows of coffering, carefully shaped to show in correct perspective only from the centre of the floor below. In each row there were twenty-eight coffers, each with a gilded rosette at its centre. Their positioning did not correspond to any vertical emphases in the drum below – given their number it could not – and this fact strengthened the impression that the dome floated gently above the drum rather than weighing heavily down on it. The way the coffering penetrated deeply into the material of the dome reinforced this impression, since its inner surface was cut away and represented only by the network of bands and ribs which separated the coffers and rose to the unbroken surface of the upper part of the dome. From here the curve swept smoothly up to the gilded cornice which ran round the vertical face of the central opening or *oculus*.

Structure

The structure of the porch is simple and traditional, in line with its appearance. Vertical columns of cut stone support horizontal entablatures of the same material and these in turn support a timber framework for the ridged roof.

For the rest of the building, the architect employed a quite different structural principle and a different material. Where cut stone is used in the rotunda its purpose is purely decorative. For example, the screens of columns which front the ground floor niches look as though they support the weight of the building above them but in fact they do not and could be removed without the building collapsing. The structural principle employed here is that of the arch and its derived forms, the vault and dome, while the material is concrete (see Appendix).

The Pantheon was built in a low-lying and marshy part of Rome and it was important to make sure that its foundations were strong and stable, so the architect began by constructing an enormous foundation ring, more than 10m. wide and 4.5m. deep, and itself made of concrete with an infill of large blocks of heavy stone (travertine) as its aggregate.

Above that the entire weight of the building was carried on the eight massive piers which stand behind the ground floor *aediculae*. These are just over 6m. thick from inside to outside but are not completely solid since they contain a number of vaulted rooms and passages up to the level of the topmost outer cornice. Semi-circular vaults, running right through the thickness of the walls from inside to out, span the niches at the level of the upper band of the drum (fig. 1.4) and so distribute the weight of the building away from the niches to the eight piers, while other vaults and arches both at

Fig. 1.4 Rome, Pantheon, structure of drum

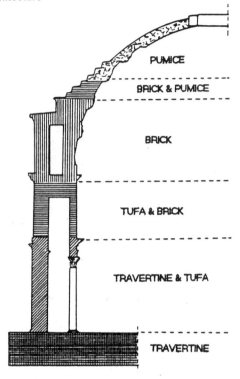

PUMICE

BRICK & PUMICE

BRICK

TUFA & BRICK

TRAVERTINE & TUFA

TRAVERTINE

Fig. 1.5 Rome, Pantheon, core materials in concrete of rotunda

this level and higher up also help in this respect. This honeycomb of internal passages was approached from stairways in the rectangular transitional block between the porch and the rotunda. The system of vaults and arches was also of great value during construction since it served to divide up the enormous task of laying the concrete filling for the drum – and so made it possible for several gangs of workers to be employed on it at the same time – and ensured stability at the most critical moment of the whole operation, when the concrete was drying into a single mass.

From inside it looks as though the dome is hemispherical and springs from the upper cornice but this is illusory (fig. 1.5). The lower part of the internal surface of the dome really forms part of the drum structure, and the dome itself is actually less than a full hemisphere and springs from the level of the topmost outer cornice. Its construction must have been extraordinarily complex. It would have been necessary first to construct a forest of scaffolding on the floor below, rising to a height of over 40m.

at the *oculus*, and then to rest upon it wooden shuttering precisely formed to reflect the eventual shape of the coffering and the smooth curve above it. The architect reduced the weight of the dome both by making it progressively thinner as it rose higher – at the *oculus* its thickness is only 1.5m. – and by using lighter aggregate in his concrete mix. He also imposed additional weight on the base of the dome, to prevent it from spreading outwards, by constructing a series of concentric stepped rings above the lower section of the outer surface. At the very top the *oculus* maintains its shape as a perfect circle in compression, with a diameter of over 8m., and helps to stabilise the whole dome.

External Appearance

The earlier section on the appearance of the rotunda dealt with it purely from the inside, and that is indeed its most important aspect. However, before returning to link the interior appearance with the structural principle, the external appearance of the rotunda deserves brief comment.

The surface of the dome was covered with gilded tiles, probably of bronze, and must have caught the eye in any distant view of this part of Rome, particularly from higher ground, but it may not have been so apparent from close at hand. The external surface of the drum now consists of the narrow bricks which formed the outer skin of the concrete mix. There is some evidence that at least the lowest band was originally covered in some way – perhaps with thin slabs of marble as on the walls of the transitional block, or perhaps with stucco – but there is no certainty as to whether the upper bands were also faced. The colonnaded forecourt, the tall pediment and the transitional block all keep the visitor's attention on the conventional facade and away from the rotunda, so that it is at least possible that they were left unfaced.

Appearance and Structure

The vast size of the rotunda, seeming almost to mock our human scale, is felt as soon as one enters it. This is partly a matter of its large dimensions: the diameter of the dome is 43.2m., larger than St Paul's Cathedral (34.5m.) or St Peter's, Rome (42.5m.) and not surpassed until the development of iron and reinforced concrete in the second half of the 19th century. Even more, however, it is a matter of its perfect proportions: the height from floor to *oculus* is exactly equal to the diameter and the height up to the upper cornice is exactly half that (21.6m.) – so that

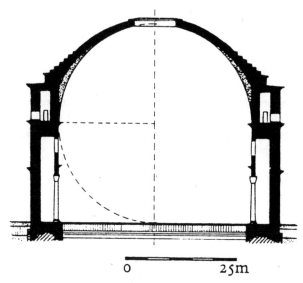

O   25m

Fig. 1.6 Rome, Pantheon, section through rotunda

a sphere with this radius could fit exactly inside the rotunda, with its lowest point just touching the centre of the floor (fig. 1.6).

Building on this scale was made possible only by what was probably the most significant development in Roman architecture, the combination of a new structural principle (the arch) with a new material (concrete). For further details of these, see Appendix.

The Pantheon has been described as 'perhaps the first great public monument...to have been designed as an interior' (J.B. Ward-Perkins, *Roman Imperial Architecture*, p. 117). Its design is dominated by the architect's vision of the interior space, and the solid mass of walls and dome, for all their rich decoration, is subordinate to that, serving only as an envelope for the real message.

The Vault of Heaven

What then is the message? It is surely linked to the name Pantheon, which has been translated as 'all holy' or 'temple of all the gods'. Dio Cassius, writing in the early 3rd century AD, records that it contained the statues of many gods and suggests this as one possible explanation of the name. He also points out that the shape of the dome resembles that of the vault of heaven, and this may be a more important clue to understanding the design. As one stands in the rotunda, the outside world is utterly cut off except for the view out through the *oculus* to the sky above, and the temple can perhaps be considered as a representation of the cosmos brought to life, like the universe itself, by the light of the sun. Some modern writers pursue this idea in greater detail, linking the seven niches of the lower band and the seven circles of the dome (five of coffering, the blank band above them and the *oculus*) with the seven planetary deities – Mercury, Mars, Venus, Jupiter, Moon, Sun, Saturn.

The first Pantheon (see next section, *Dating*) was rectangular, so if Dio Cassius' suggestion is correct, the credit for this sophisticated concept belongs to the architect who designed the present Pantheon during the reign of the Emperor Hadrian (AD 117-38). The design certainly fits a period when the hold of the traditional gods was beginning to wane, new religions such as Christianity and Mithraism were spreading, and an interest in more abstract powers such as Fortune was developing. It also suits the personality of Hadrian himself, a man of strong and restless intellectual passions which included both religion and architecture.

Dating

Yet the inscription on the entablature of the porch makes no mention of Hadrian. It reads:

M. AGRIPPA L.F. COS. TERTIUM FECIT

(Marcus Agrippa, son of Lucius, built this in his third consulship).

Agrippa was one of the chief supporters of the first emperor, Augustus, and died over a hundred years before the start of Hadrian's reign. From other sources we know that Agrippa was responsible for many buildings, including a Pantheon on the same site as the present temple. We know too that this building was destroyed in a major fire in AD 80, rebuilt soon after, and again severely damaged in AD 110. We must also consider a statement in a 4th century AD biography of Hadrian that he 'restored the Pantheon'. Why then are architectural historians so sure that the Pantheon dates from the reign of Hadrian?

In the first place, there are two pieces of negative evidence. Agrippa's Pantheon was rectangular and its porch faced south – the opposite direction to the present building – and the mastery of concrete vaulting shown in the rotunda would have been beyond the architects of Agrippa's time. Beyond these, however, examination of the building has revealed that all parts of it were constructed at the same time, while a detailed study of the date stamps on the bricks which face the drum proves that the Pantheon was an entirely Hadrianic building, started early in his reign in AD 118 or 119 and dedicated some time between AD 125 and 128. Finally, the same biographer who spoke of Hadrian's 'restoration' provides an explanation for his mistake. He also records that although Hadrian was responsible for a huge number of buildings in all parts of the empire, he did not put his name on any of them except the temple of his father, the deified Trajan.

Survival

The Pantheon was soon recognised as one of the most impressive buildings in Rome. It became an essential stop on the tourist circuit, and the historian Ammianus Marcellinus, recording a visit to the city by the Emperor Constantius II in AD 357, described it as a 'vaulted region'. By then Constantinople had replaced Rome as capital of the empire and the decline in prosperity caused by this shift began to threaten the preservation of major buildings. What saved the Pantheon was the decision in AD 609 that it should become a church.

From then on its survival was secured by the protection of the popes, though not without certain accidents along the way. In AD 663, for example, the Emperor Constans II took away the gilded bronze tiles from the dome roof, while almost a thousand years later Pope Urban VIII is said to have removed two hundred tons of bronze from the porch roof and used it to make cannon to protect his fortress of Castel Sant' Angelo – which had itself started life as Hadrian's Mausoleum.

Minor alterations were also made to its appearance. Towards the end of the 13th century AD a bell tower was built above the centre of the pediment. This remained until early in the 17th century AD when it was replaced by two lantern towers on either side of the transitional block between porch and rotunda. These were not removed until the 1880s and so appear in early photographs. Internally, the major change was to the decoration of the upper band of the drum in the 1740s. Apart from a small area where the original has been restored, this remains in place.

Perfectest of all the Antiquities?

Yet for all its qualities one aspect of the Pantheon has often been thought less than successful: the relation of porch to transitional block and of transitional block to rotunda. As one looks at the temple from the front, the most obvious signs of this are the artificial pediment on the transitional block and the unusually steep and heavy pediment over the porch; from the side, the lack of continuity between the cornice of the porch and those of the rotunda (fig. 1.1). At one time architectural historians used to explain these features by suggesting that they had been built at different periods but the definite establishment of a date in Hadrian's reign for the entire building has ruled out explanations along these lines. A different type of explanation has recently been proposed (Davies, Hemsoll and Wilson Jones, 'The Pantheon: Triumph of Rome or Triumph of Compromise?' *Art History* Vol.10, No. 2).

Briefly, the authors suggest that the design of the porch underwent major change after the construction of the temple had started, its columns being reduced in height from an originally intended 60 Roman feet (17.7m.) to the current 50 Roman feet (14.75m.). 60 ft columns would have brought the gable of the porch up to the same height as the transitional block, so eliminating the awkward upper pediment, and would have been in better proportion with the steep pediment. As they would also have been proportionately thicker, the spacing between the porch columns, unusually wide in the Pantheon as built, would have approximated more closely to the standard (fig. 1.7 A). From the side,

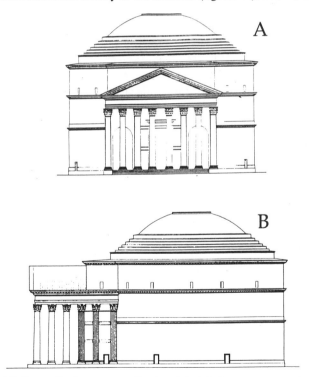

Fig. 1.7 Rome, Pantheon, suggestion for original design

the main cornice of the rotunda would have been continuous with the single cornice of the porch and transitional block (fig. 1.7 B). There are also a number of other anomalies, less apparent to the casual eye but revealed by careful study of the measurements, which can be removed by the assumption that the original design of the Pantheon porch envisaged 60 ft columns.

However, if the decision to reduce the size of the columns resulted in a less coherent building, it cannot have been taken willingly and must have been forced on the architect by circumstances outside his control. It is impossible to be sure what these were, but one suggestion is simply that it proved difficult to acquire sufficient of the larger columns. Columns, particularly monoliths like those in the Pantheon porch, seem to have been produced in standard sizes. 60 ft was the largest of these and columns of this size were used only rarely and for buildings of great importance. Special arrangements would have to have been made for quarrying the shafts in Egypt and transporting them to Rome. The Pantheon was not the only building project with which Hadrian was involved at the time. The temple dedicated to his predecessor, the deified Trajan, was being built at the same time as the Pantheon and it too had a facade of eight 60 ft monoliths of Egyptian granite. If Hadrian's architects were faced with a shortage of column shafts, they would have had to choose between the two projects. It would have shown a dangerous lack of political tact and *pietas* if Hadrian had set his own project above the duty he owed his predecessor. His only real choice, then, was whether to leave the Pantheon unfinished until sufficient 60 ft columns could be assembled – and this might have meant a delay of several years – or to order his architects to use the more readily available 50 ft columns and make what adjustments to the original plan seemed necessary. Given the over-riding importance of the interior of the Pantheon, this might well have seemed a price worth paying.

Whether or not this theory eventually wins general acceptance, it is worth consideration both for its intrinsic interest and for the way it shows that the study of Roman architecture is not just a matter of learning a series of established facts but one that contains a number of important questions which are still unanswered.

Chapter 2
Approaching Architecture

What is Architecture? (a) Utility and Aesthetics

A bicycle shed is a building; Lincoln Cathedral is a piece of architecture. Nearly everything that encloses space on a scale sufficient for a human being to move in is a building; the term architecture applies only to buildings designed with a view to aesthetic appeal.

This is Nikolaus Pevsner's answer, in the Introduction to his *Outline of European Architecture*, and a glance at the illustrations to that book show that he concentrates on churches, cathedrals, castles, palaces, public buildings and the homes of the well-to-do. Only when he reaches the 19th and 20th centuries does he begin to give much attention to factories, offices or the homes of the less prosperous.

Yet works on Roman architecture regularly include plans and illustrations of structures which would fall outside Pevsner's definition: housing blocks, warehouses, roads, bridges and, perhaps most obviously, aqueducts. The most famous aqueduct is probably the Pont du Gard near Nîmes in southern France (fig. 2.1, see next page), about which Sir Ian Richmond wrote:

The aesthetic effect is due solely to the functional design and aptly illustrates the sheer elegance of straightforward engineering. ('Architecture and Engineering' in *Roman Civilization*, ed. J.P.V.D. Balsdon).

Both writers are examining the relation between utility and aesthetics and are seeking to judge buildings in the light of some balance between them – though note the distinction between Pevsner's 'with a view to' and Richmond's 'effect'. One complication in trying to assess them is that each generation learns from its predecessor and what may have originated as a purely utilitarian solution to a purely practical problem may be taken up by later generations both for its functional value and for its aesthetic appeal.

Fig. 2.1 Nîmes, Pont du Gard

Our third witness comes from Rome and his statement emphasises the social value of structures. In AD 97 Sextus Iulius Frontinus was appointed *curator aquarum*, superintendent of the water supply for the city of Rome. In his book *On the Aqueducts* he wrote:

> Contrast the numerous and essential structures which bring so much water into the city with the idle pyramids or the famous but useless monuments of the Greeks (*de Aquaeductis*, 16).

It is worth noting that in Roman times the distinction between architect, builder and engineer was by no means as clear cut as it is today. The only surviving book by a Roman architect, Vitruvius' *de Architectura*, deals not only with town planning and the design of houses, temples, theatres and other public buildings but also with the qualities of different materials, with hydraulics, with the construction of artillery and siege machines and with the manufacture of sundials. Vitruvius' own view neatly combined the functional and the aesthetic: he believed buildings should be constructed with an eye to strength, utility and beauty (1.3.2). Another famous architect, Apollodorus of Damascus, showed similar versatility. He built a bridge over the Danube for the armies of the Emperor Trajan, wrote a treatise on *Engines of War*, and was responsible for one of the most ambitious building projects of imperial Rome, the Forum and Markets of Trajan (fig. 3.13 B & C). The Forum, with its basilica, libraries and Trajan's Column, was built largely of

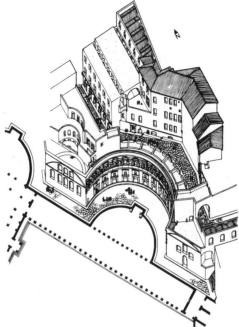

Fig. 2.2 Rome, Trajan's Markets, axonometric view

marble on the traditional 'post and lintel' structural principle we have already seen in the Pantheon porch and it was clearly designed 'with a view to aesthetic appeal'. The Markets (fig. 2.2) are quite different: although part of the same project they are utilitarian in spirit and are built of brick-faced concrete on the vaulted principle. Yet it is the latter style which only twenty years later made possible the aesthetic vision of the architect of the Pantheon.

In dealing with the Romans, therefore, it is best to work with a fairly broad definition of what counts as architecture.

What is Architecture? (b) Space and Mass

A second approach to this question lies in the attempt to identify the quality which distinguishes architecture from the other visual arts, painting and sculpture. In general there is little disagreement about this – Pevsner, for example, talks about spatial quality, Edmund N. Bacon (*Design of Cities*) about the interrelation between mass and space – but there is a risk that this may seem only a cliché, too obvious to be helpful. It becomes useful, however, if we examine the relative importance of Bacon's two terms in different periods and styles of architecture. Greek architecture, for example, was an architecture of mass, with the emphasis placed firmly on the structural elements of a building. With the Romans, on the other hand, the focus of architectural thought was on the use of space to express the essential function of a building or group of buildings. This was true both of individual buildings, like the great imperial *thermae* with their logically planned sequence of rooms of different shapes and for different purposes, and of the relations between buildings, as in the forum of a city or a temple precinct.

Why is Architecture Important?

It provides us with spaces for all our functions and activities, particularly those which involve us as members of the community. This is perhaps most obvious when we consider types of building: home, office, factory, shop, school and college, hospital, law court and prison, football stadium or theatre, barracks, pub, church and crematorium – we have a mental image for each of them. Yet the same specialisation of space applies both on a smaller scale within buildings and on a larger one in the relation between them. We recognise the difference in function between stage and auditorium in a theatre, or between production line and office in a factory, largely through architectural distinctions – distinctions of shape, scale and materials – while if we were suddenly dropped by parachute in an unknown city, we should still be able to tell whether we had landed in the civic centre or a residential area. We have a vocabulary of shapes and plans which allows us to understand the world in which we live and so to take part in debate about its preservation or reform. Moreover, comparison of the dominant building types in different societies – the church in the Middle Ages, for example, municipal government buildings in the Victorian period, out-of-town shopping centres perhaps in the early 1990s – is one of the keys to understanding those societies and the values by which they live.

> The building of cities is one of man's greatest achievements. The form of his city has been and always will be a pitiless indicator of the state of his civilization. (Bacon, *Design of Cities*)

How does architecture affect us?

In fact, architecture is inescapable: we live in architecture and respond instinctively to it. Its appeal is mainly to the eye but other senses are not excluded. We notice the difference between the sounds of a meat market, for example, or a busy street and those of a quieter area like a residential square or a university campus, and if we run through in our mind a route across a town or city we know well, we can recall it as a pattern of different types and levels of sound. Even our sense of touch can be involved as we move from paved streets to cobbles or to the grass of a park.

Consider how much information is presented to us within a single street. Few streets are absolutely flat and absolutely straight. If a street drops steeply away, we may be able to see out over the roofs below to the country beyond; the buildings at the top of a concave slope seem to loom over us as we climb up, while on a convex one they may not even be visible until we are almost upon them. Similarly, a curving street sometimes reveals what lies ahead, sometimes hides it. The frontages may be consistent – in height, in style, in material – or vary. Some buildings may project into the pavement; at other points there may be a break in the building line to accommodate an open space – a square perhaps or a churchyard. Junctions with other streets may be marked by some special feature – a roundabout with a fountain in the centre or a group of statuary – or may come upon us almost by surprise. A sudden narrowing of street and pavement, an increase in the height of the frontages may draw us on and make us quicken our step; a broadening out, a drop in the building level opposite may allow the sun to reach our side of the street and may encourage us to slow down, relax and look about us.

None of these possibilities is always right or always wrong: harmonious regularity can be restful or boring; jagged variety, exciting or confusing. The street will mean different things to different people, even to the same person at different times, and buildings do not each convey a single fixed message to those who use them or pass by them. In this respect architecture is like the other arts. The way we understand the meaning of a novel or a play, for example, is always personal, depending on a dialogue between what the author presents to us in his work and what we bring to it from our individual experience of life and literature.

Chapter 3
Town Planning

(a) The Development of Cities

Aosta

The city of Aosta (Augusta Praetoria) lies in north-west Italy at the foot of the St Bernard passes. The Greek geographer Strabo described the circumstances of its foundation in the course of Roman campaigns against the Gallic tribe of the Salassi in 24 BC:

> 8,000 fighting men were counted and 3,000 other Salassians, in addition to the 6,000 already mentioned. Terentius Varro, the general responsible for their defeat, sold them all into slavery. Augustus Caesar sent out 3,000 Romans and founded the city of Augusta Praetoria on the spot where Varro had camped. Now the whole region is at peace as far as the passes over the Alps. (Strabo, 4.7.205-6)

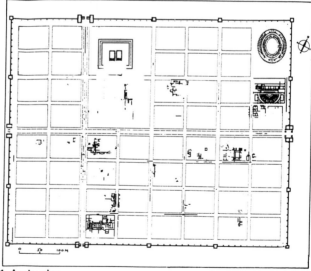

Fig. 3.1 Aosta, plan

The military aspect of this foundation is clear from the severe regularity of its plan (fig. 3.1). Its rectangular shape is contained by defensive walls, there is a single gate on each side and the grid of its streets is almost unbroken. Aosta is an extreme, and hence untypical, example of such regularity but the grid plan was a standard feature of Roman town planning and one that was particularly common in the north-western provinces of the empire.

The Grid Plan: Origins and Advantages

However, the grid plan was not a purely Roman discovery. Its earliest traces in Italy can be found in some of the Greek cities founded in the southern part of the peninsula in the 7th and 6th centuries BC. At Poseidonia – later known by its Latin name, Paestum – the grid (fig. 3.2) consists of long narrow blocks separated by three main streets in one direction and more than thirty minor ones crossing them at right angles, with a strip of land in the middle set aside for public buildings. In this form it dates from just before 500 BC, but the basic plan may have been established when the city was founded in the previous century.

Under Greek influence the principle of grid planning was also taken up by the Etruscans, the dominant power in north and central Italy in the 6th century BC. Marzabotto, just south of Bologna, has a formal grid of streets crossing each other at right angles. Spina, in the marshy land of the Po delta, is also formally planned, though here – as much later in Venice – canals take the place of streets. Both date from about 500 BC.

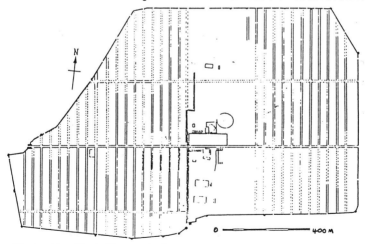

Fig. 3.2 Poseidonia (Paestum), plan

What all these examples – Greek, Etruscan, Roman – have in common is that they are all new foundations established on 'green field' sites. In that kind of situation grid planning had several advantages. Everyone involved in the new enterprise would have understood the total picture from the start, including the important matter of the position of the main public buildings – for local government, religion, entertainment; they would have been able to work rapidly and even to start work simultaneously in different parts of the city without risk of confusion; and even in the very early days they would have enjoyed a feeling of completeness and security important to settlers in a new and potentially dangerous area.

Colonisation under the Romans

By the time Aosta was founded the Romans had already had more than three hundred years' experience of founding new cities, often in territory where peace was not yet firmly established. Many of these were colonies, and their original function is well summarised by the historian Appian in the 2nd century AD:

> As success in war brought the Romans control of parts of Italy, they used to take part of the land and either founded cities on it or sent out settlers from their own population to cities already in existence. They regarded these colonies as garrisons. (*Civil War*, 1.1.7)

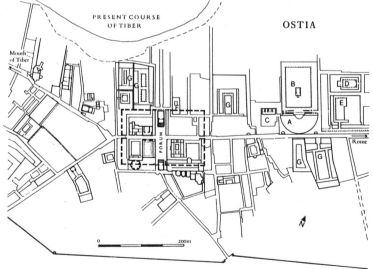

Fig. 3.3 Ostia, plan

Ostia was quite probably the first, founded about 340 BC to protect the mouth of the Tiber. The original colony became the nucleus of the later city and can be seen outlined by the broken line on the plan (fig. 3.3). Like Aosta, it was strictly regular, the rectangular shape being divided into four equal sections by the two main streets, the *cardo maximus* (north-south) and the *decumanus maximus* (east-west), and with a space in the centre which later became the forum. The flat land at the mouth of the Tiber lent itself easily to grid-planning but the Roman liking for this type of lay-out can also be seen in the very different conditions of Cosa (fig. 3.4). The colony here was founded in 273 BC on a steep uneven promontory overlooking the coast of Etruria and the perimeter was irregular, but within that there is a grid of streets and a forum with public buildings down one side.

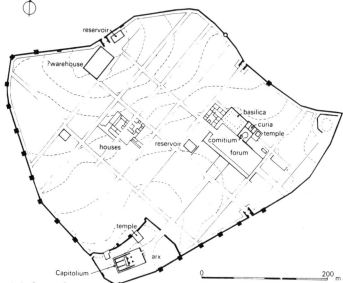

Fig. 3.4 Cosa, plan

The North-Western Provinces

Roman power continued to expand: first across the Apennines and into the Po valley, where the modern street plans of cities such as Piacenza and Como still provide evidence of their foundation, and then across the Alps.

Here the Romans entered an area with little tradition of city life. Along the French Riviera and the Catalan coast of Spain there were a few Greek foundations, notably Marseilles, and further south in Spain a scattering of Phoenician settlements, but beyond the coastal strip their influence was limited. The Roman annexation of Gallia Narbonensis in 121 BC and the foundation of a colony at Narbonne provided another stimulus for urbanisation, but when Julius Caesar began his Gallic campaigns in 58 BC the basic form of political organisation in north-west Europe was still the tribe, not the city. Caesar's description of the level of urban development in Britain,

> The Britons call it a town (*oppidum*) when they fortify an impenetrable area of woodland with a rampart and a ditch (*Gallic War*, 5.21),

must have been equally true of large parts of the north-western provinces of the empire.

The most important step in the development of cities in this area came towards the end of the 1st century BC with two major programmes of colonial foundations, those of Julius Caesar and Augustus. Both had built up large armies in the course of the Civil Wars and one of their main motives was to reward their veterans by giving them a grant of land as a form of pension. Caesar is credited with founding more than 30 colonies, Augustus with around 75. By the end of Augustus' reign there were eight or nine cities in Gaul which ranked as full Roman colonies and as many again with the lower status of Latin colonies. They were concentrated in Provence and the Rhône valley, were built on the grid pattern and had the usual range of Roman public buildings. They provided a model for urban development further north, both for new foundations like the large and prosperous city of Autun (Augustodunum) and for additions and improvements to sites already under occupation such as Bourges and Besançon.

Architects and Government Service

By the 1st century BC the profession of architect was well established in Rome. Vitruvius (7, Preface) refers to some of his predecessors by name and lists a large number of technical treatises both in Greek and Latin. Some architects worked in private practice – Cicero makes fun of one he had employed who used to make a parade of his learning to baffle his critics (*Letters to Atticus*, 2.3) – but opportunities were also widely available in the public service and particularly in the army. The brief information Vitruvius gives about his own career reveals that he served as a military architect-cum-engineer under Julius Caesar and Augustus. One of his projects for the latter was to design a basilica and shrine for the colony he founded at Fano.

Architects serving in or attached to the army remained important whenever new colonies were founded and must also have provided advice and technical assistance with the planning of other new towns like the tribal capitals (Paris and Autun, for example, in France, Leicester and Caerwent in Britain). We know that the Romans regarded the development of cities as perhaps the most effective way of consolidating their rule in the provinces. In the biography he wrote of his father-in-law Agricola (Governor of Britain, AD 78-84), Tacitus put this with a typical combination of clarity and cynicism:

> At this stage the Britons lived an uncivilised life in scattered communities and were naturally warlike. To help them develop a liking for peace and quiet, Agricola encouraged individuals and assisted communities to build temples, fora and houses in the Roman style...Gradually the Britons were drawn to all that makes vice attractive, porticoes, baths and elegant banquets. In their folly they called all this civilisation, though really it was just part of their slavery. (*Agricola*, 21)

An inscription from the forum at St Albans (Verulamium) records the dedication of the basilica by Agricola in AD 79.

In the north-western parts of the empire, then, the stimulus for the growth of cities was incorporation in the Roman empire, and a map of modern Europe shows how succcessful the process was. Paris, Lyons, Bordeaux, Strasbourg, Cologne, Mainz, Coblenz, Barcelona, Valencia, Saragossa, London, York, Lancaster – these are merely a small sample from the much longer list of cities founded by the Romans.

The Eastern Provinces

The position in the eastern part of the empire was very different. Here the Romans came into contact with societies which already possessed many flourishing cities, some of them with histories going back hundreds of years before their incorporation in the Roman empire. In the Greek world the basic political unit had long been the *polis*, an independent city with a surrounding rural area, and the philosopher Aristotle had simply taken it for granted that this was the natural way to live, the only form of social organisation which permitted humans to realize their potential:

> The *polis* originated to ensure the necessities of life; its continued existence is to ensure a happy life. (*Politics*, 1252b)

Towards the end of the 4th century BC Alexander the Great, formerly one of Aristotle's students, overthrew the power of the Persians and established an empire which stretched briefly from the Mediterranean to Afghanistan and India. He and his successors founded many new cities as centres of Greek life and culture, the most famous being Alexandria in Egypt.

In the east, therefore, it is comparatively rare to find a completely new Roman foundation. Generally it was a matter of adding new quarters and particularly Roman types of building, e.g. baths, to cities which already existed. A good example is Athens itself, where in about AD 130 a handsome arch, put up in honour of the Emperor Hadrian to celebrate the new districts he was building, records on one side 'This is Athens, the ancient city of Theseus' and on the other 'This is the city of Hadrian, not of Theseus'.

Dugga and Timgad

The contrast between these different traditions can be illustrated by examining two cities in North Africa.

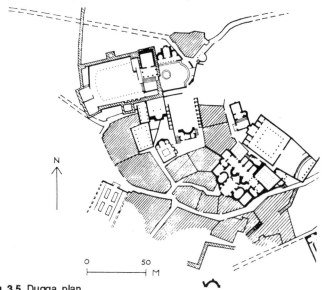

N

o ├──────────┤ M
      50

Fig. 3.5 Dugga, plan

Dugga in Tunisia was originally a native settlement but then came under the influence of Carthage, on the coast some sixty miles to the north-east, before being incorporated in the Roman province of Africa. Its plan (fig. 3.5) clearly reveals both the unplanned, winding streets, passages and stairways of the native city (no grid plan here) and the inclusion within and around them of the typical elements of a Roman city: forum, temples in the Roman style, monumental arches, theatre and a large symmetrically planned baths establishment.

Timgad in Algeria lies about 200 miles west of Dugga but even a glance at its plan (fig. 3.6) shows that this is a city that was formally planned from the outset. It was founded in AD 100 by the Emperor Trajan and was intended for legionary veterans from the nearby fort at Lambaesis. From Lambaesis too came the architects responsible for its planning. It is almost square and has a regular grid of streets within the walls with spaces set aside for forum and basilica and for the theatre. Soon after its foundation, the Capitolium was built outside the walls – a sign

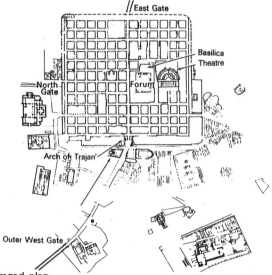

Fig. 3.6 Timgad, plan

perhaps of its early success in attracting a large population; not long after that the Baths outside the North Gate were built, the walls around the south-west corner were taken down and the area covered with housing, and a number of seemingly unplanned developments grew up outside the walls. By the end of the 2nd century AD, as the outer gates to east and west indicate, the city had increased greatly in size. For all its rigidly military foundation Timgad soon had an attractive range of urban amenities, including – as well as forum and theatre – twelve public baths, markets, a library, a splendid triumphal arch and streets shaded by porticoes.

Timgad, therefore, stands as a good example of a planned city and of the continuing importance of military architects but also as a reminder that cities are living entities which develop and change over time.

The same process can also be seen elsewhere.

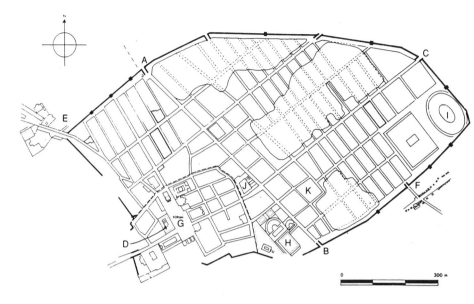

Fig. 3.7 Pompeii, plan

Pompeii and Ostia

Both Pompeii and Ostia illustrate the way a small settlement could
expand outside its original limits.

At Pompeii (fig. 3.7) the original settlement occupied only the
south-western corner of the later city but by at least the middle of the 3rd
century BC, and perhaps a good deal earlier, a much larger area was
enclosed by a new set of walls. Within this circuit several different grids
can be distinguished, and this may be evidence that they were developed
at different dates. Between the earliest nucleus and the main north-south
road running from the Vesuvian Gate to the Stabian Gate [A-B] there are
irregular blocks of buildings, while immediately to its east large squarish
blocks seem to be aligned on it. Further east again, blocks of a narrower,
rectangular shape are based on the main east-west road leading from
the forum to the Sarno Gate [C]. Finally, in the north-west corner of
the city the blocks run parallel to the sanctuary wall of the Temple of
Apollo [D], which is believed to pre-date the lay-out of the forum in
the 2nd century BC.

Ostia (fig. 3.3) soon began to expand outside the walls of the original
settlement. Irregular developments along the lines of the approach roads can

be seen very clearly to the west and south of this nucleus. Then, in about 80 BC, came the construction of a new circuit of walls, enclosing an area of about the same size as Pompeii (65 hectares). In one important respect, however, Ostia was different from Pompeii. Its role as the main harbour for Rome gave it considerable importance and in the 1st century BC the north-eastern quarter of the city was declared public property and replanned on a regular pattern. The theatre with its colonnaded square [A, B] and the four temples neatly ranked side by side at the back of a shared courtyard [C] form part of this programme, while important later buildings such as the Headquarters of the Vigiles [D] (Fire Brigade) and the Baths of Neptune [E] fit in with it.

Leptis Magna

Leptis Magna in Libya (fig. 3.8) was much larger than Pompeii or Ostia and eventually became one of the wealthiest cities of the empire. Starting as a Phoenician trading station, probably in the 7th century BC, it first came into contact with Rome during the Punic Wars and was incorporated in the empire towards the end of the 1st century BC.

Few traces remain of the Phoenician settlement. The general line of Roman development is from the area of the Old Forum [A] near the harbour along the line of the main road to the interior. Among the earliest

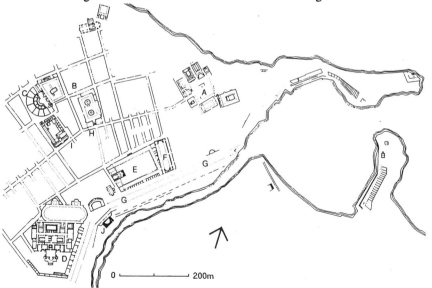

Fig. 3.8 Leptis Magna, plan

buildings in Roman style were a row of three temples on the north-western side of the Old Forum, a market [B], and the theatre [C]. In the mid-1st century AD the streets were paved, a basilica was built opposite the three temples and the Old Forum itself was repaved and surrounded on three sides by a portico. Even when the city expanded inland, building and restoration continued in this area. Three more temples were added on the south west side of the Old Forum between c. AD 71 and 153, while in the mid-2nd century AD a curia was built next to the basilica and the facades of two of the earlier temples and the forum porticoes were rebuilt in marble. The development of the Old Forum thus extended over nearly two hundred years but at every stage of the process it had a coherent architectural identity.

The growing prosperity of Leptis was marked in AD 110 by its promotion to the status of colony. Inscriptions mention a Forum and Basilica of Trajan which must have been built at about this time. Their location has not been discovered but they probably lay in the still unexcavated part of the city, perhaps beside the road leading to the West Gate. Another indication of the importance of Leptis at this time was the construction in AD 127 of the Baths of Hadrian [D]. These are the earliest example outside Rome of the symmetrical 'imperial' baths which were coming into fashion in the capital and they also mark the date at which imported marble replaced local limestone for the public buildings of Leptis.

The third main phase in the development of Leptis is associated with Septimius Severus, a native of the city who became emperor in AD 193. The buildings he founded in Leptis are among the richest and most elaborate to be found anywhere in the empire. To the east of the 1st century AD grid, he built a forum and basilica (E, F, & fig. 3.9), the

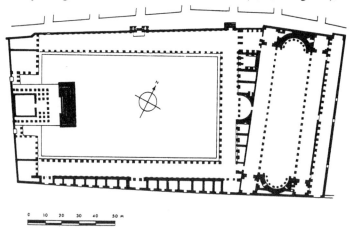

Fig. 3.9 Leptis Magna, Forum & Basilica of Septimus Severus, plan

former focused on an impressive temple, the latter influenced by the basilica from Trajan's Forum in Rome. The site these occupied was irregular but the architects took great care to ensure the internal symmetry of both sections. His second main contribution was a huge colonnaded street [G], more than 40m. wide and stretching some 400m. from the harbour inland past his new forum and basilica.

Public Benefactors

Few cities could claim an emperor among their citizens, but the kind of generosity Septimius Severus showed towards his native city differed only in degree from what happened elsewhere. Prominent citizens in all parts of the empire saw it as part of their duty (unofficial perhaps but clearly recognized for all that) to donate public buildings to their cities. This was not pure generosity, of course: the prestige they acquired by their gifts would prove helpful in their political ambitions. In Leptis itself, for example, the market and the theatre were both put up at the expense of Annobal Rufus – whose first name reveals that he came of a Phoenician family and his second that he had acquired Roman citizenship. At Pompeii, the Crispi Pansae, father and son, funded restoration work in the amphitheatre after the earthquake of AD 62, while the rich freedman, N. Popidius Ampliatus, paid for repair work to the temple of Isis in the name of his six-year old son, and so secured his election at this unreasonably early age to the ranks of the town council.

(b) Elements of a Roman City

So far this chapter has concentrated on the development and general appearance of Roman cities. It is now time to consider the main types of public building a traveller in, say, the 2nd century AD would have found in a Roman city.

Approaching the City

The traveller would have passed first through a city of the dead, for the cemeteries of Roman towns stood outside their walls. At Pompeii groups of 'tombs' can be seen outside the Herculaneum and Nuceria Gates (fig. 3.7 E, F), though the word is misleading since these are much larger than we are familiar with from the cemeteries of our own towns. They are small buildings, often with a decorated burial chamber set in a small courtyard and sometimes of two storeys. At Rome itself they are even larger and more elaborate: the Via Appia was lined with tombs for ten miles outside the city, among them that of Caecilia Metella which took the form of a round tower on a square base and stood more than 20m. high, while a representation of an oven stood in a fine position just outside the Porta Maggiore to commemorate the baker Eurysaces. The spirit of ostentation which was the motive for such tombs is satirised in Petronius' *Satyricon*, where the nouveau riche Trimalchio says:

> You'll build my tomb according to my instructions?. . .It must be 100ft wide across the front and stretch back for 200ft from the road. I want fruit trees of all kinds and an abundance of vines planted round my ashes. It's daft to have elaborate houses while we're alive and not to worry about the place where we shall live much longer. . .And make sure you carve some ships on it, with their sails bellying in the wind, and put me sitting on a dais, in my official robe and with my five gold rings, distributing cash in public. (*Satyricon*, 71)

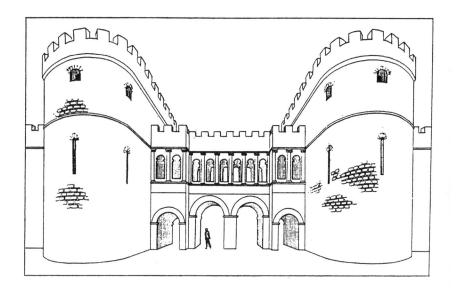

Fig. 3.10 Autun, Porte Saint-André

Next came the city gate, set in a powerful wall with towers projecting at intervals on either side. Vitruvius (1.5.5) explains the advantages of round towers over rectangular ones: battering rams can easily destroy the exposed angles of the latter but have little effect on the former – they operate as horizontal arches. Gates differed in design. Some of those at Pompeii consisted of a single arch, but often they were more elaborate: the Porte Saint-André at Autun had two central arches for vehicles flanked by two lower ones for pedestrians and was crowned by an arcaded gallery (fig. 3.10). Walls and gates had an obvious defensive function but also an important symbolic one: they were one of the architectural features which most clearly distinguished a real city from a mere settlement and were designed to impress on the visitor the status and prestige of the city he was approaching. A city with walls was a Rome in miniature.

As the quotation from Frontinus in Chapter 2 (p. 14) indicates, the Romans prided themselves on ensuring an abundant water supply for their cities, and the engineering works to achieve this would sometimes also have been apparent from the roads approaching a city. The most obvious example is Rome. By the early 2nd century AD the capital was served by ten aqueducts, several of them originating more than 60km. away. One of the most important, the Aqua Marcia, entered the city 20m. above ground level; for the last 15km. of its course it had been carried across the countryside on continuous arches. Pompeii by contrast relied upon wells for its water supply until the reign of the Emperor Augustus, when it was linked to the aqueduct which also supplied Naples and Herculaneum. The Pompeian branch of this aqueduct entered the town near the Vesuvius Gate and ran straight into a distribution tank. From there water was taken off in three branches to the street corner fountains on which most of the inhabitants relied for drinking water, to the public baths and lavatories, and to some of the private houses. However, aqueducts carried on arches were expensive to build and to maintain and were only constructed when there was no simpler alternative. Usually the water supply reached cities in a channel set at ground level or buried slightly below it. At Autun, for example, two wholly subterranean aqueducts are known, one just over 6km. and the other nearly 4km. long, while the water supply for Wroxeter (Viroconium) ran at ground level in an open channel for just over 1km.

Inside the City

Inside the walls lay all the other major types of public building the traveller would have expected to find: temples, commercial buildings,

buildings for local government and those for the entertainment of the citizens. (See Chapter 4.) What remains for this chapter is to consider two elements which may at first seem hardly to count as architecture, since they are spaces rather than buildings, the forum and the streets. They merit inclusion, however, because they were not simply neutral gaps between the buildings but made their own positive contribution to the dialogue of the city and were deliberately designed to do so.

Forum

The forum was the centre of community life. In cities that developed naturally, it was probably in origin simply an open space, kept free of private buildings and reserved for public use of all kinds – commercial, judicial, religious, political, social, as market, parade ground, polling booth, census station, gladiatorial arena. In a city that was formally planned, like Aosta or Timgad, the setting aside of a space for the forum and the construction of the buildings which were to surround it were likely to be part of the original plan, though one subject to modification as time went on and needs, or fashions, changed.

  At Augst (Augusta Rauricorum), overlooking the Rhine near Basel, it was nearly 200 years after its foundation in 43 BC before the forum complex was complete in permanent form (fig. 3.11). Here the

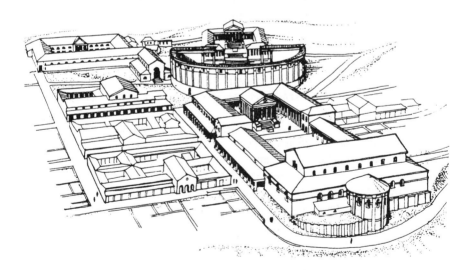

Fig. 3.11 Augst, Forum complex

forum was divided into two parts by the *cardo maximus*. At the far end stood a temple, facing out across the central open space to the basilica at the near end, and the whole area was bound together by the colonnades that surrounded it.

As city life became more sophisticated, the character of the forum changed and the range of activities in it became narrower. Specialist accommodation was provided for actors and gladiators and separate markets were established for the different categories of foodstuff, especially those involving messy operations such as slaughtering. (Rome had specialist markets for the sale of cattle, pigs, fish, vegetables, and slaves.) The activities which always remained important were those concerned with the administration of justice and local government.

The typical forum was usually rectangular. Vitruvius (5.1.2) recommended a proportion of 3:2 for length:breadth, but this was far from uniform. (At Timgad the forum was nearly square, while at Pompeii with a proportion of nearly 4:1 it was unusually long and thin.) It was surrounded by a colonnade, frequently of two storeys, which provided shady walkways with a view out over the forum at ground and first floor level, and the ground level of the open central area was usually set one or two steps lower than the base of the surrounding colonnade. The effect of this was to mark off the forum from the rest of the city – it was often a pedestrianised area – and to convert it from just an open space into a formal court, a kind of unroofed room. Napoleon's description of the Piazza San Marco in Venice as the 'finest drawing room in Europe' parallels the sensation one would have felt in the forum of a major Roman city.

Pompeii: the Forum

A description of the forum at Pompeii just before the earthquake of AD 62 illustrates many of these points (figs 3.7 G, 3.12). Its basic lay-out had been established towards the end of the 2nd century BC. At the north end stood a temple. Raised on a high podium and with the strong vertical emphasis of its Corinthian columns and steep pediment echoed by the shape of Vesuvius beyond it, this dominated the forum and provided a strong visual axis along its length. Its dedication to the 'Capitoline triad' (Jupiter, Juno, Minerva) marked the fact that for all its Oscan and Greek origins Pompeii was now a truly Roman town. Down the two sides and across the southern end ran a two-storey colonnade (Tuscan below, unfluted Ionic above) which gave a feeling of cohesion and enclosure to the forum. Work began on replacing the original tufa columns in limestone during the reign of Augustus but the task was still incomplete.

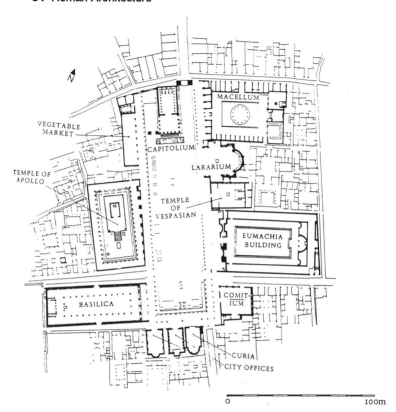

Fig. 3.12 Pompeii, Forum, plan

At the southern end was a group of buildings concerned with the administration of the city. The oldest and grandest of these was the basilica, a large aisled hall which served as commercial centre, law court and meeting place for the citizens; next came three smaller buildings for the chief magistrates (*duoviri*) and their assistants (*aediles*) and the curia for meetings of the town council; finally, in the south east corner was an unroofed but enclosed area usually identified as the *comitium* (voting station) but which may in fact have been the law court.

Most of the western side was taken up by the wall of the courtyard surrounding the Temple of Apollo. North of this were a market building possibly for grain or vegetables, and in the corner beyond it a public latrine.

The two largest buildings on the eastern side both had a mainly commercial function but should not be thought of as purely utilitarian in design. Both, for example, are set obliquely to the forum, aligned on streets leading out to the rest of the town, but in both cases the architects have

ensured that they present a facade which is parallel to the forum colonnades and so reinforces its basic north-south axis. The *macellum* in the
north-east corner was a meat and fish market. Its rectangular courtyard is
surrounded by small shops, while in the centre stands a twelve-sided *tholos*
roofed with a dome and containing a water tank linked to the city sewers.
(This became a standard element in the design of markets and another, more
elaborate, example can be seen at Leptis.) What distinguishes the building
is that its columns are of finely carved Carrara marble, a luxury stone only
just coming into use during the reign of Augustus when the *macellum* was
built. Further south, the Eumachia Building was the Headquarters of the
Clothworkers, the main guild or trade association in Pompeii. Its facade was
set unusually far back so that one could take in the pattern of rectangular and
curved niches either side of the wide central door and appreciate the details
of its marble facing – spirals of acanthus leaves around the door and a double
order of marble columns, the stone for some imported from North Africa,
Greece and Asia Minor. Both buildings also had a religious element. At the
back of the *macellum* was the meeting place of the *Augustales*, the priests
who celebrated the cult of the imperial family, while the Eumachia Building
was dedicated to the *Concordia Augusta et Pietas*, represented by Livia, the
deified wife of Augustus.

Rome: the Imperial Fora; Forum of Augustus

The process of specialisation mentioned above was taken furthest in
Rome itself. There, in an area north of the original forum, the *forum
Romanum*, five new fora were constructed between about 50 BC and AD
120 (fig. 3.13, see next page), the emperors clearing aside existing
buildings or digging back into the flanks of the Quirinal Hill to secure
the space they needed for their new designs. These 'imperial fora'
completely lacked the commercial activity and informal socialising
characteristic of the forum at Pompeii or Augst; their function was to
celebrate the power and increase the prestige of the emperors responsible
for their creation. They differed in detail but all shared three features
important in Roman planning: a strong sense of enclosure, axial design
and rich decoration. In addition, they were all conservative in material
and structure. The Romans continued to regard cut stone, especially
marble, and the post and lintel system as the natural choice for prestige
public developments.

The forum of Augustus (fig. 3.13 A), completed in 2 BC, was in effect
a grandiose temple precinct. A formal entrance led into it from the south-
west and directly opposite on the long axis and placed on a high podium was

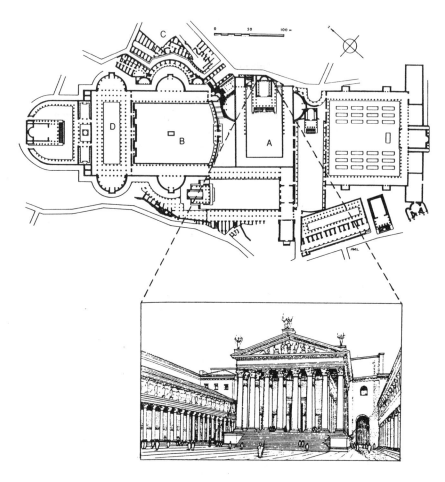

Fig. 3.13 Rome, Imperial Fora & Temple of Mars Ultor

the Temple of Mars the Avenger. (Augustus had vowed the temple forty years earlier when he defeated the assassins of his adoptive father, Julius Caesar.) Down either side of the courtyard stretched a tall colonnade. On the outer side of the two colonnades at a point level with the top of the steps leading up to the temple were two large semi-circular recesses. These created a cross-axis, though one that is probably more apparent from the plan than it was on the ground. All this was completely symmetrical, but this was only achieved by careful planning within an irregular site. Behind the temple a wall, 35m. high and built partly of fireproof stone from Gabii, divided the forum from the slum dwellings outside. The temple itself was built of Carrara marble, while for the forum and its colonnades coloured marbles from Greece, North Africa and Turkey were also used. The quality of the architectural carving is extremely high and many of the craftsmen probably came from the Greek world. Above all, the forum was the setting for a rich and meticulously worked out programme of sculpture. At the focal point where the two axes crossed stood a statue of Augustus himself. Above him in the pediment and in the interior of the temple were his divine ancestors: Mars (father of Romulus, the first king of Rome), Venus (mother of Aeneas and through him ancestress of the Julian family) and Julius Caesar himself (now formally regarded as a god and so entitled Divus Iulius). In the centre of the two recesses, facing out towards Augustus, were Aeneas and Romulus and flanking these and extending down the colonnades were statues of the great figures of the Roman past, mythical and historical, each carrying a brief summary of his achievements. Almost in the centre of the couryard was another statue of Augustus, dressed as a triumphant general and riding in a chariot drawn by four horses which carried the legend *Pater Patriae* (Father of his Country). The message all this conveyed to the Romans who visited the forum was that Augustus was not – as some might mistakenly have remembered – a revolutionary who had gained power after long and bitter civil wars but a legitimate ruler who stood at the culminating point of Roman history and embodied all its virtues and achievements.

Streetscape

The back streets of Pompeii or Ostia were plain and functional: blank walls broken only by an occasional entrance rise directly from the sidewalk or even from the paving of the street itself. They connect one part of the city with another efficiently enough but do little to raise the spirit. Often, however, the streets of Roman cities – particularly, of course, the main thoroughfares linking the gates, the forum and the main public buildings – were full of architectural character and made an exhilarating contribution to the experience of urban living.

Such streets usually had a raised sidewalk on either side and these were often shaded by porticoes projecting from the building line and setting up a lively pattern of light and shade as the sun moved round. The most elaborate examples are found in North Africa (Septimius Severus' colonnaded street at Leptis has already been mentioned) and in the eastern parts of the empire. At Jerash (Gerasa), in Jordan, (fig. 3.14) the *cardo maximus* ran for 800m in a straight line through the middle of the city and

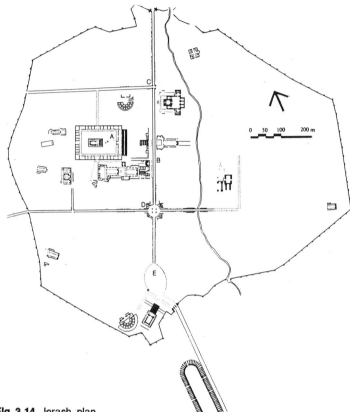

Fig. 3.14 Jerash, plan

was divided into three sections of roughly equal length by the two main cross streets. These were all lined with continuous colonnades, a feature which had the effect of binding together the different quarters of the city but which was handled with sufficient flexibility to avoid monotony. The spacing of the columns, for instance, or the height of the entablature could be varied to emphasise particular buildings, such as the approach to the Temple of Artemis [A] or the Nymphaeum [B]. The two main crossing points were also marked out by special architectural features. At the point where the *cardo* crossed the north *decumanus* [C] traffic would have passed under a four-way triumphal arch, while the crossing with the south *decumanus* [D] was distinguished by a *tetrakionion* standing in a circular piazza (fig. 3.15). These features 'punctuated' the message of the *cardo*, breaking it up into shorter lengths and so making it more intelligible.

Particular attention was also given to changes of direction. The unusual 'oval piazza' at Jerash [E] was probably designed to accommodate the change in alignment between the *cardo maximus* and the already existing street entering the city through the south gate. From whichever direction one approached, the curve of its Ionic colonnade would have carried the eye smoothly round to the next stage of one's journey. Two other solutions to the problem of reconciling different alignments can be seen at Leptis (fig. 3.8). One occurs about halfway along the *cardo maximus* as it runs inland from the Old Forum, where a triumphal arch [H] and a four-way arch [I] bracket a slight change of direction. The other comes at the point where Septimius Severus' colonnaded street met the previously existing street beside the palaestra of the Baths of Hadrian. On the inner (east) side of the junction stands a large Nymphaeum [J], a fountain with an elaborate architectural backdrop of superimposed columns separated by niches and statues. On the opposite side, next to the convex wall of the palaestra, was a concave segmental recess [K]. What might so easily have been just a rather awkward junction thus became one of the focal points of city life, where the richness of red granite and cipollino (a strongly veined marble, white to pale green in colour) combined with the play of light on the water to create a pleasant place to relax and talk with one's friends.

Finally, we should not forget the second population of a Roman city: the statues of prominent citizens and benefactors, found mainly in the fora and other open spaces, which gave physical appearance to the history of the city and bound past and present together in a continuing process.

Fig. 3.15 Jerash, Tetrakionion

Chapter 4
Public Architecture

(a) Religion: The Temple

The Greek and Italian Traditions

Fig. 4.1 shows the Temple of Hephaistos, built in Athens between about 450 and 420 BC; fig. 4.2, the Maison Carrée (Temple of Rome and

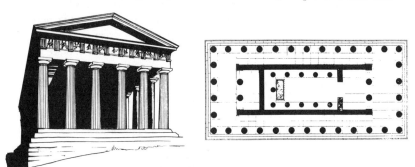

Fig. 4.1 Athens, Hephaisteion
[Courtesy of D. Yarwood, *The Architecture of Europe*, Batsford, London, 1974]

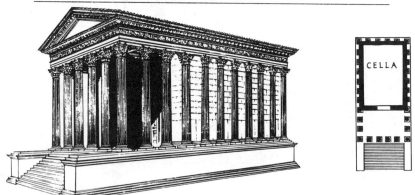

Fig. 4.2 Nîmes, Maison Carrée, entablature
[Courtesy of D. Yarwood, *The Architecture of Europe*, Batsford, London, 1974]

40

Augustus) built at Nîmes (Nemausus) in southern France in AD 1-2. The two share a certain family resemblance: both are rectangular, both have a ridge roof with pedimental gables at either end, and both of course have columns. Yet there are also major differences: for example, the Maison Carrée stands on a tall podium and can be approached only from the front, it does not have a complete peristyle like the Hephaisteion, and there is a deep porch at the front before one reaches the entrance to the *cella*. The influence of Greek temple architecture on the Maison Carrée is clear, but what is the source of these other features?

The Romans were greatly influenced in religious matters by the Etruscans. One important practice they adopted from them was that of taking the auspices, interpreting the will of the gods by observing the flight of birds. This was no haphazard affair. The priest or magistrate stood on a designated spot in front of the temple with the building behind him and marked out an area of the sky ahead as the sacred space for observation – this was, in fact, what the Latin word *templum* originally signified. A position with a clear view was essential – hence the importance of the high podium – and the whole ceremony emphasised the front of the temple.

The earliest Roman temple of which any traces remain is the Capitolium, the temple of Jupiter, Juno and Minerva on the Capitol in Rome. According to tradition this was built in the final years of the monarchy, when the Etruscan Tarquinius Superbus was king in Rome, and dedicated in the first year of the Republic (509 BC). It has the high podium and frontal emphasis identified above as non-Greek features and exemplifies what Vitruvius (4.7) described as the Tuscan temple. However, for detailed examination of this type it is better to take a later and better preserved example.

Cosa: the Capitolium

The Capitolum at Cosa (figs 3.4, 4.3) was built in the middle of the 2nd century BC, rather over a hundred years after the colony was founded. It **Fig. 4.3** Cosa, Capitolium stands on the highest point of the site, in a magnificent position looking down over the city towards the forum and the public buildings, while immediately behind it the hill drops steeply away to the sea below.

The ground was first built up to provide a level terrace supported by a wall of roughly shaped stone. This formed the basis for the podium itself, some 3.7m. high, whose side walls projected forward to enclose the broad flight of steps leading up to the porch and so emphasised the frontality of the design. The back and side walls of the temple were blank but at the front was a deep porch with a facade of four widely spaced Tuscan columns. The porch, whose inner half was flanked by extensions of the *cella* walls, provided a transition from light to darkness as one entered the temple, and the triple *cella* housed the statues of the three divinities who made up the Capitoline triad.

Outside, the steep gable roof jutted forward over the top of the steps and on either side were widely projecting eaves designed to throw rain water well clear of the footings of the walls, an important concern when so many of the early temples were made of sun-dried brick. The superstructure, corresponding to the entablature of a Greek temple, was of wood (the gaps between the columns of the porch were too wide for stone beams) and so was the framework of the roof under its terracotta tiles. The decorative elements were also of terracotta, often richly moulded, always brightly coloured and already showing considerable Greek influence: antefixes above the eaves, plaques covering the exposed sides of the wooden beams, decorations standing up like a crest along the gable edges, and the figures in the pediment.

A visitor coming to Cosa from the Greek world soon after the Capitolium was completed might have found it rather unsophisticated in design and rough in execution but would have had to acknowledge the direct power with which it defined the sacred space in front of it and dominated activity there.

Almost contemporaneously with the Capitolium at Cosa, a new temple was built which signalled an increase in Greek influence. In 146 BC, Q. Metellus returned to Rome from campaigning in Greece and commissioned the temple of Jupiter Stator from the Greek architect Hermodorus of Salamis. This was the first temple in Rome to be built of marble – presumably imported from Greece – and had a colonnade down the sides but not across the back, a compromise between Greek and Italian ideas. The combination of Italian plan and volume with Greek orders and decoration soon became standard in Italy and spread later to the major cities of at least the western empire. The Maison Carrée at Nîmes is a good example.

Nîmes: the Maison Carrée

The Maison Carrée (fig. 4.2) stands in a squarish courtyard, with a single-storey colonnade at the back and on either side, and faces north over the forum, which is about 1m. lower than the temple courtyard. It shares with the Capitolium at Cosa the typically Italian high podium and deep porch but the total effect is very different. Why is this? One main reason is that whereas at Cosa the outer walls of the *cella* are blank and the use of columns is limited to the porch, the Maison Carrée seems at first glance to have a colonnade all round. A closer look reveals that this is an illusion: only the porch has free-standing columns; down the sides and across the back the columns are engaged, i.e. set into the wall behind. This device serves to bind together front, sides and rear of the building and, despite the way the temple dominates the forum, to diminish somewhat the frontal emphasis. It is no accident that, like Greek temples, the Maison Carrée is often illustrated in three-quarter view.

This sense of the building as a coherent whole is strengthened when one considers a second difference between the two temples. At Cosa the terracotta decoration is concentrated at the front; in the Maison Carrée the rich programme of architectural carving, in a good quality local limestone, runs all round the building in a series of horizontal courses at the level of the entablature (fig. 4.4). A third feature which is likely to strike anyone looking at the temple is the V-shaped channelling which spreads in a grid across the walls. The channels usually occur where two blocks of stone meet but sometimes they are merely a surface feature cut across the middle of a single block to preserve the regularity of the grid. Their purpose is purely decorative: in the bright sunlight of Mediterranean France they create a shifting pattern of light and shade and so bring the inert mass of the wall to life. The fact that the architect gave the engaged columns a rather pronounced profile by making them slightly more than a strict half-circle shows how much importance he attached to this factor. The focus of design for the Maison Carrée was exterior appearance.

Fig. 4.4 Nîmes, Maison Carrée, entablature
[Courtesy of D. Yarwood, *The Architecture of Europe*, Batsford, London, 1974]

In this respect it contrasts strongly with the 2nd century AD Pantheon, and indeed with the general tendency of Roman architecture, but it dates from a period when Greek influence on the architecture of Rome was particularly strong and several of its features resemble work in the capital. In plan, for instance, it is a miniature version of the Temple of Apollo in Circo (c. 20 BC), the acanthus scroll on the frieze recalls the Ara Pacis (9 BC), and the Corinthian capitals and channelled masonry are similar to those on the Temple of Mars the Avenger in the Forum of Augustus (2 BC). These resemblances and the evident importance of the Maison Carrée are the basis for the suggestion that the architect and craftsmen came from Rome. However, the extreme variety of detailing (none of the capitals and very few of the flowers on the underside of the cornice are identical) and the stylistic development from the back of the temple, where work probably started, towards a freer and more confident handling at the front, point rather to the use of local craftsmen and possibly to a local architect working on the basis of plans from Rome.

(b) Administration: The Basilica

The Romans were only able to control their huge empire by devolving considerable powers to smaller, more local, units. Cities and towns had recognised judicial and administrative responsibilities and developed a range of buildings to deal with them. The most important of these was the basilica which was always prominently sited, in line with Vitruvius' recommendation (5.1), beside the forum.

The word 'basilica' is Greek – it means kingly or royal – and in origin the basilica may have owed something to the stoas and peristyles of contemporary Hellenistic cities, but it developed into a character-istically Roman type of building. The former, however elaborate, were essentially subordinate to the open space they surrounded, whereas the focus of the basilica was its own interior and in this it shared the emphasis on interior space we have already seen in the Pantheon. The stimulus for this development may have been the need to provide a suitable 'envelope' for a range of functions. One of these was to serve as a kind of exchange or dealing centre for businessmen; Vitruvius is so concerned for their comfort that he says the basilica should be built in the warmest corner of the forum so that they do not get cold in winter! Another – and the combination may strike us as odd – is as a magistrates' court; again Vitruvius provides evidence for this when he explains how, in the basilica he designed for the Augustan colony of Fano, he included a recess for this purpose so that those appearing before the magistrate should not get in the way of the businessmen in the main hall of the basilica.

Pompeii: The Basilica

In 184 BC the Basilica Porcia was built in the main forum of Rome, shortly followed by two other examples of this new type of building, but the earliest which we can study at all easily is the basilica built in the south-western corner of the forum at Pompeii towards the end of the century (fig. 3.12). A colonnaded porch with a lean-to roof fronted the forum end of this building, providing access to the basilica proper through five doors, three set between Ionic columns and one in the wall to either side of them. Inside, a peristyle of 28 giant order columns, arranged 12 x 4, marked out the central space from the surrounding aisles and supported the timber framework of the roof. Down the side walls engaged Ionic columns stood opposite those of the giant order and probably helped to support a gallery over the side aisles. (Fig. 4.5 shows a cross-section through the four columns at the end of the central space.) Between them the walls were stuccoed and painted to imitate coloured marbles and above were Corinthian columns, their lower halves engaged

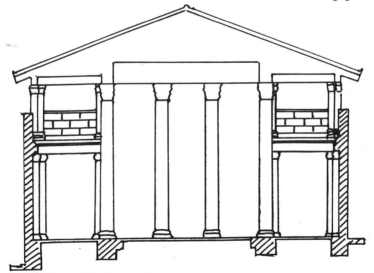

Fig. 4.5 Pompeii, Basilica, section

in the side walls but above that standing free to create large unglazed windows which lit the interior. (One uncertainty that remains is whether the giant order columns were Ionic or Corinthian. In favour of the former is that they shared with the definitely Ionic columns of the entrance wall the same relatively unusual method of construction: they had a rubble centre faced with irregular pieces of brick; this was then fluted and covered with stucco. Against that, their capitals would have stood at the same height as the definitely Corinthian capitals of the side aisles.) At the far, western, end of the building a two-storey tribunal jutted out from the rear wall, leaving rectangular recesses on either side. It had a facade of Corinthian columns and was crowned with a pediment. Presumably it served as the centre for the work of the city magistrates, while the main body of the hall was occupied by the merchants, bankers and other businessmen upon whom the prosperity of the city was founded.

The tribunal went some way to establishing a longitudinal axis, but its effect was reduced by the cross wings of the giant colonnade since this would have prevented a clear view of the tribunal from almost anywhere in the building. The plan thus represented something of a compromise between the centrally focused Greek peristyle and the Italian liking for axial planning. Despite this, the scale of the building – the interior columns are about 13m. high and the roof timbers over the central nave span 14m. – together with its light-filled interior and richly carved and painted detailing made the basilica a most impressive addition to the range of public buildings in Pompeii. It is good evidence for the wealth and architectural sophistication of provincial Italian cities at this time.

Rome: The Basilica Ulpia

The basilica at Pompeii is placed end on to the forum but basilicas with their long side facing the forum were also common. This was the case with the three early examples in the *forum Romanum*, with the basilica at Cosa and with the one Vitruvius built at Fano (5.1.6-10). The spread of urbanisation in northern Italy and in the north-western provinces has been mentioned in the previous chapter. In this area one pattern almost became standard: the basilica occupied the entire space at one end of the forum, often – as at Augst (fig. 3.11) – facing a temple at the other end. The position of the basilica in these cases parallels that of the head-quarters building (*principia*) of a legionary fort and reminds us that the architects were drawing on a shared set of planning assumptions whether they were working in civil or military practice. The most splendid example of this type is the Basilica Ulpia in Trajan's Forum in Rome (fig. 3.13 D). Almost a hundred years later, it was the dominant influence in the design of the basilica Septimius Severus built at one end of his forum in Leptis Magna (fig. 3.9) and it also enjoyed a profitable after-life as the model for the basilican churches of early Christian Rome.

Rome: The Basilica Nova

The Basilica Ulpia, however impressive for its size and rich decoration, is still a traditional building, made of cut stone and designed on the post and lintel principle. The first basilica to exploit the possibilities of concrete vaulting was also one of the last buildings of Classical Rome, the Basilica Nova (fig. 4.6), started by Maxentius in AD 307 and completed, with alterations, by his rival and successor Constantine I.

The Basilica Nova stands alongside the Sacred Way in the *forum Romanum*, where the massive vaults of its north-east side aisle still survive to dominate the area. Its ground plan is not dissimilar to that of earlier basilicas (a central nave flanked by side aisles), but its closest resemblance is to the *frigidaria* of the great imperial *thermae*, such as the Baths of Caracalla or those of Diocletian, which had only just been completed. The nave is composed of three bays, roofed by cross vaults springing from the entablature above enormous Corinthian columns and lit by lunette windows filling the space cut out by the intersection of the

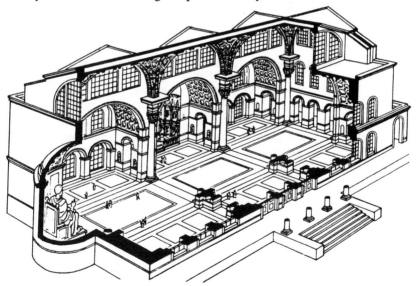

Fig. 4.6 Rome, Basilica Nova, interior

vaults with the side and end walls. It is buttressed by the side aisles, each composed of three barrel vaults set transversely to the main axis. As originally planned, the entrance was at the south-east end and the longitudinal emphasis was reinforced by the presence of a large statue of Maxentius in a vaulted apse at the other end. Constantine altered the feel of the building by placing the main entrance mid-way along the south-west side and adding an apse to the central vault on the opposite side for his own statue.

The inside of the building was richly decorated with a patterned floor of marble slabs, coloured marble facing to the lower part of the walls and stucco above that, and deep coffering to the vaults of both nave and aisles. Yet all this is subordinate in effect to its sheer scale – the nave alone covers an area of 80m. x 25m. and rises to a height of 35m. at the top of the vaulting – and this in turn is made possible only by the mastery the Romans had acquired in the use of concrete vaulting.

Vitruvius wrote at a time before this mastery has been achieved and from a conservative point of view, but he would surely have recognised that the Basilica Nova satisfied his demand for a combination of strength, utility and beauty.

(c) Entertainment

(i) Theatres

Drama was the first literary genre to reach maturity in Rome – the traditional date for Livius Andronicus' first play is 240 BC and Plautus was active before 200 BC – but the first permanent theatre in Rome was not built until 55 BC. Until then the Romans made do with temporary structures, put up for the particular occasion on which they were required and then taken down again. Though made mainly of wood, these temporary theatres could be surprisingly elaborate. The most striking example is the one erected by M. Aemilius Scaurus when he was aedile in 58 BC. According to Pliny the Elder (*Natural History*, 36.114-6), the wall at the back of the stage consisted of three storeys: the lowest of marble (though Pliny does not say whether this was in solid blocks or just a veneer), the middle one of glass (perhaps a covering of glass-paste mosaic), the uppermost made of wood and then gilded; it was faced with 360 marble columns with 3000 bronze statues between them. We may recognise a touch of exaggeration in Pliny's account but at least it allows us to appreciate the force of a comment reported by Tacitus (*Annals*, 14.21), that it was less expensive to have a permanent theatre than to build a temporary one every year and then demolish it.

Outside Rome, indeed, though temporary theatres are known to have existed and appear frequently in vase paintings from southern Italy, permanent theatres built of stone started much earlier. Some, like the one at Gabii, which probably dates from the mid-2nd century BC, formed part of a temple complex and their main function must have been to provide a performance space for the rituals involving music and dance that were associated with the cult. Others, like the theatre at Pompeii, built in the first half of the 2nd century BC, had no obvious religious context but were civic buildings forming one of the amenities of urban life. Both these examples were relatively close to Rome, but educated Romans were also likely to have travelled abroad and seen the long-established permanent theatres in the cities of Greece and Asia Minor.

The Roman Theatre: Orange

The typical Greek theatre, such as Epidauros (fig. 4.7 A), consisted of two separate parts: an area for the spectators, rather more than a semi-circle in shape and resting upon a hillside, and a low stage building. In performance they were linked visually by the circular *orchestra* where the chorus performed, but structurally they were quite distinct, kept apart by the unroofed entrances (*parodoi*) on either side, and from their seats the spectators could look out over the stage building to the country-side beyond.

Roman theatres were based upon the Greek model – the word 'theatre' comes from the Greek verb meaning 'to watch' – but the differences are significant and illustrate some of the general tendencies of Roman architecture. The theatre at Orange (Arausio) (fig. 4.7 B), built in the second half of the 2nd century AD, provides a good example. To begin with, the Roman theatre was essentially a single structure.

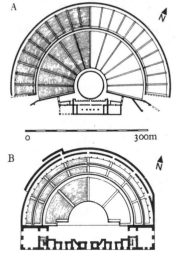

Fig. 4.7 Greek & Roman Theatres, plan

Stage building and auditorium were pulled together by a continuous perimeter wall, and instead of open *parodoi* there were vaulted passages over which at least the upper rows of seats continued. To achieve this tighter structural organisation, the auditorium and *orchestra* were limited to a semi-circle, the latter losing its function as a performance space and becoming instead the place where individual seats were put out for the most important members of the audience.

Two other features reinforced the feeling of enclosure. Over the stage a wooden roof served both to protect the performers from the weather and as a soundboard to project their voices forward, while the audience was shaded from the sun by canvas awnings suspended from wooden masts rising above the perimeter wall.

A second important characteristic was the rich interior decoration, centred as in Scaurus' temporary theatre on the *scaenae frons* (fig. 4.8, Jerash), the wall at the back of the stage. Here, a screen of columns two or three storeys high was arranged in an intricate pattern of projections and recesses, of curved and rectilinear shapes, and yet further enriched with statues. The play of light and shade caused by the movement of the sun would have helped to bring this architectural pattern to life.

Lastly, although Roman architects often built their theatres against a hillside – it was after all the cheapest solution – they were not limited to this type of position and possessed in the arch and vault a technique which made it possible for them to build up the substructure on flat ground if they wished.

Fig. 4.8 Jerash, South Theatre, scaenae frons

Vitruvius devotes more space to theatres (5.3-9) than to any other type of building except temples. His account of how to design a theatre (5.6) is so precise that a reader with ruler and compasses can draw it out on paper, but he also deals at some length with the siting of theatres and the question of their acoustics. Finally, he refers to the importance of equipping the theatre with colonnades where the spectators can walk about or take refuge if a sudden shower of rain interrupts the performance. Sometimes, as at Orange, there is a colonnade running round the top of the auditorium. Elsewhere, a colonnaded square is laid out behind the rear wall of the stage. Colonnades of this type can be seen at Pompeii (fig. 3.7 H) and Ostia (fig. 3.3 B) but in both cases these developed an additional or an alternative function. At Pompeii the colonnaded square was taken over as a training school for gladiators, while at Ostia the small rooms round the outside of the square were used as offices for the shippers from the different ports which traded with Ostia.

(ii) Amphitheatres

One of the best known 'facts' about the Romans is that they revelled in blood-thirsty sports, fights to the death between gladiators or between man and beast, and the Colosseum is probably the most widely recognised of all Roman buildings. Yet Vitruvius does not mention amphitheatres. One reason for this is that although amphitheatres existed in other parts of Italy, the first permanent one in Rome, that of Statilius Taurus, was not built until about 30 BC when Vitruvius' architectural education was already complete. However, this cannot be the whole explanation since much the same was true of theatres and yet, as we have seen, Vitruvius gives them considerable attention. What makes the difference is that gladiatorial contests were a specifically Italian activity, developing perhaps from the funeral rites of the Etruscans and particularly popular in Campania, and their omission from his work shows that Vitruvius was writing in a cultural tradition stemming from the Greek world, where gladiatorial games were never as popular.

Pompeii: The Amphitheatre

The first permanent amphitheatre to survive is the one at Pompeii, which was built probably in 70 BC, soon after the city became a colony and received a settlement of legionary veterans as a form of penalty for its opposition to Rome in the Social War and as security for its future good behaviour. It was sited in the extreme south-east corner of the city in an area that was still not built up and was convenient to the city gates (fig. 3.7 I). This was an important point since the capacity of the amphitheatre was about 20,000 – well over the total population of Pompeii – and so visitors from neighbouring towns must have been expected.

It has what became the standard oval shape and measures about 135m. by 105m.. The arena and the two tiers of seating closest to it were dug down below ground level and the earth excavated for this was then piled up to form the solid banking which supported the seats of the third tier. Except for the south-eastern section where it rested directly against the city wall, the earth banking was surrounded by a thick retaining wall of concrete faced in *opus incertum* (see Appendix). The wall sloped inwards towards the top and was strengthened by radial buttresses linked to each other at the top by arches, on top of which a broad walk ran round the amphitheatre and linked up with the city walls. On days when there were shows in the arena the spaces between the buttresses provided a good position for traders to set out their food and drink stalls for the spectators.

Entrance to the arena was by tunnels sloping down from ground level at either end, though the one at the south end had to take an awkward bend to the west to come out clear of the city wall. From these tunnels, vaulted passages ran round between the lowest and the middle tiers of seating and gave access to them. Access to the third tier was by external staircases set against the retaining wall and thence by the walk round the top of the arcades. This also allowed spectators to reach a superstructure of additional seating added to the main building during the final years before the eruption of Vesuvius and possibly reserved for women under legislation of the Emperor Augustus. The seating throughout was originally of wood but by AD 79 about half of it had been replaced in stone.

The major functional disadvantage of the amphitheatre at Pompeii is that because of the relative scarcity of entrances and exits it would have taken a long time for spectators to assemble and reach their seats at the beginning or to disperse at the end of a show. Experience at major football grounds shows how dangerous these moments can be if there are rival gangs of supporters, and an incident of this kind occurred at Pompeii in AD 59, between fans from Pompeii and some from Nuceria, a small town about ten miles further inland. Tacitus (*Annals*, 14.17) describes how jeering and taunting led first to stone-throwing and eventually to the use of swords; the Pompeians had the better of things and several of the Nucerians were killed or severely wounded. After an investigation by the consuls, the Senate decreed that the city authorities of Pompeii should be banned from putting on gladiatorial shows for a

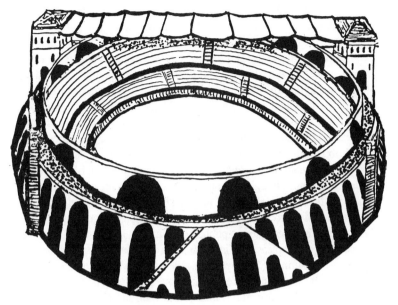

Fig. 4.9 Pompeii, Amphitheatre

period of ten years and that the sponsor of the show and his associates should be exiled. The above illustration (fig. 4.9) gives a good impression of the amphitheatre with its paired external staircases and the awning shading the spectators.

Rome: The Colosseum

The popularity and importance of gladiatorial and wild beast shows steadily increased. One indication of the popularity some gladiators could enjoy comes from graffiti on the walls of Pompeii, where Celadus is described as the girls' heart-throb and Crescens, more frankly, as the master who gives the girls their nightly medicine. A second is the growth in the number of gladiators employed, from three pairs in 264 BC, the first occasion on which gladiators were seen in Rome, to 320 pairs in 65 BC and a total of 10,000 individuals in AD 107 when Trajan celebrated his victory in the Dacian Wars. It is also recorded that 5,000 beasts were killed at the inauguration of the Colosseum in AD 80 – and the 19th century Italian archaeologist Lanciani gives a graphic account of how his men dug through into the black, viscous, fetid remains of one of the pits into which the carcasses were thrown. Lastly, we should note that by the middle of the 1st century AD Rome enjoyed nearly 160 days holiday each year – though there were, of course, no weekend breaks – and games of one kind or another were celebrated on more than ninety of these.

Writing in about AD 120, the satirist Juvenal laments that the Roman mob has forgotten the political role it once enjoyed and is interested only in *panem et circenses* (*Satires*, 10.81), its diet of bread and public entertainments, both provided by the emperors and one of the chief means by which they controlled the volatile populace of the city. Statilius Taurus' amphitheatre had been destroyed in the great fire of AD 64 and about ten years later the Emperor Vespasian decided to replace it on a larger scale. His Amphitheatrum Flavianum, more often known as the Colosseum, though the source of the name is uncertain, stood in a shallow depression which had previously been the site of the lake in the gardens of Nero's Golden House, and Vespasian could therefore claim that he had dedicated to public entertainment an area that Nero had reserved for private pleasure. The Colosseum was the largest amphitheatre ever built, measuring 188m. by 156m. externally and rising to a height of over 48m. The whole structure stands upon a massive foundation ring of concrete capped with travertine blocks, 51m. wide and 12m. deep.

The fundamental difference between the amphitheatre at Pompeii and the Colosseum is that the seating for the latter is not built upon solid banking but upon an artificial framework (fig. 4.10), a honeycomb of corridors, stairways and ramps separated by piers of load-bearing

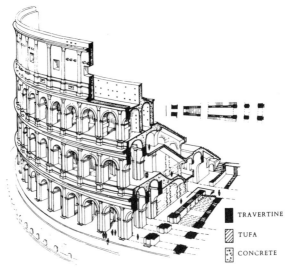

TRAVERTINE

TUFA

CONCRETE

Fig. 4.10 Rome, Colosseum, section

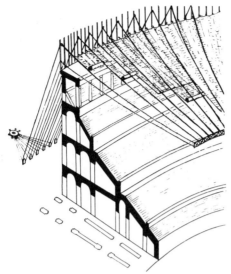

Fig. 4.11 Rome, Colosseum, sectional view & awnings

masonry. Most of what lies below the narrow skin that carries the actual seating is in fact empty space: at ground level this consists of two systems of barrel-vaulted corridors – four concentric rings around the arena and eighty cutting through these along the radii of the oval. Between them rise piers of travertine stone, linked at the top by concrete vaults and with screen walls of tufa between them. (For the differences between these materials, see Appendix.) Investigation has shown that, once the foundations had been laid, the next stage was to complete the travertine framework and, after that, four gangs worked simultaneously on the tufa and concrete sections and on the timberwork.

Up to the top of the third storey, the seating was of marble, since its weight could be buttressed by at least the outer ring corridor (fig. 4.11). Above that, where the seating rested against the outer wall, it was important to reduce the weight and the seats of the top level were made of wood. As in a theatre, the spectators were shielded from the sun by awnings. The supports for the 240 masts which carried these can still be seen in places towards the top of the outer wall, as can some of the bollards to which the ropes were attached. A detachment of a hundred sailors from the imperial fleet was quartered nearby to superintend the operation of this system.

Another difference from the amphitheatre at Pompeii can be seen in the arena itself. At Pompeii it is solid, whereas here it consists of a carefully constructed and ingenious set of corridors and cages designed

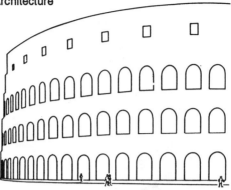

Fig. 4.12 Rome, Colosseum, exterior without engaged columns

to ensure that wild beasts could be brought in below ground level and then lifted up to the actual arena with minimum danger to their handlers. If Suetonius' statement (*Titus* 7.3) is true, that the Colosseum was flooded for a mock naval battle as part of the opening ceremonies, this elaborate system must have been constructed in the reign of Domitian, after the formal inauguration.

In external appearance, the Colosseum resembled the outer wall of the auditorium of a free-standing theatre. Except at the two ends and in the centre of the two sides where there were elaborate porches, it was fairly plain, a uniform pattern of arches flanked by engaged columns on the first three storeys and a plainer wall with pilasters above that. The columns at ground level were Tuscan, and above that in a sequence that became standard came Ionic and Corinthian. The plain walls of the attic storey had shallow Corinthian pilasters and were broken by large square windows in every other bay, alternating with shields of gilded bronze. The use of the orders here was purely decorative and had no structural function. The engaged columns enlivened the facade by creating a more marked pattern of light and shade. They also broke up the daunting mass of the total building into more manageable sections and so gave it something of a human scale (compare fig. 4.12, which shows what the building might have looked like without the engaged columns, with fig. 4.10).

Finally, by drawing attention to the entrances, they emphasised the purpose of the structure. A spectator's ticket would tell him which of the seventy-six numbered entrances he should use to reach the particular wedge of seats and the particular level where he had been assigned a place. The capacity of the Colosseum was about 50,000 (Wembley Stadium holds 126,000) and the elaborate system of corridors and stairways was superbly designed to permit relatively trouble-free access and dispersal (fig. 4.13). It is a triumph of functional design.

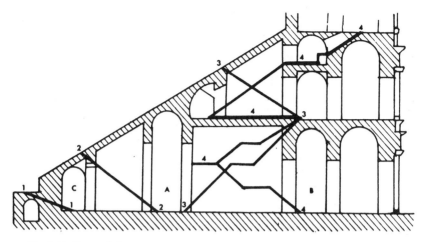

Fig. 4.13 Rome, Colosseum, system of stairways & corridors

(iii) Baths

It is easy to find parallels in the modern world for temple, basilica, theatre and amphitheatre but we have nothing quite like the great *thermae*, or public baths, of imperial Rome, which provided facilities not just for personal hygiene but also for a bewildering range of social, cultural and sporting activities within a single establishment.

Seneca (*Epistulae Morales*, 86) describes the tiny, dark bath house which the great Scipio Africanus had in his house at Liternum and contrasts it with the extravagance of his own day. Such simplicity may well have remained true for some time of baths in private houses, but from at least the 2nd century BC public baths provided as an amenity for the entire commmunity were relatively sophisticated in design and decoration.

Pompeii: the Stabian Baths

The Stabian Baths (figs 3.7 J, 4.14) occupied an irregular site east of the forum and close to the main north-south road through the city. Their earliest part was the range of small hip baths [A] in the north-western corner of the site, which may possibly date back to the 4th century BC. They were placed close to a deep well in the street outside from which water was lifted by human or animal power to a reservoir at first floor level, and this remained the sole source of water for the baths until Pompeii received its aqueduct supply. However, the most important

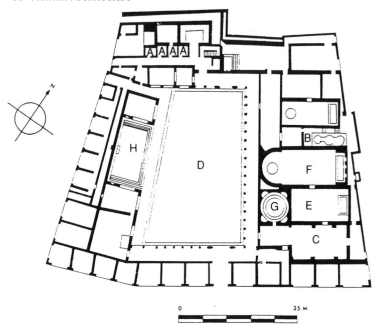

Fig. 4.14 Pompeii, Stabian Baths, plan

stage in the development of these baths came in the second half of the 2nd century BC, at about the same time as the basilica was being built.

Two new sets of rooms were then built on the east side of the *palaestra*, the men's baths at the south end and the women's to the north. A furnace [B] placed between the two hot rooms served both sets, heating not only the water but also the air circulating under the floor and in pipes up the walls. A man visiting the baths would enter a small lobby giving access to the *apodyterium* [C], where he would leave his clothes. From there he could either go out to the *palaestra* [D] for some vigorous exercise or straight into the actual bathing rooms, each of a different temperature. Though dark, these were elegant rooms, with mosaic floors and stucco decoration on walls and ceilings. The *apodyterium, tepidarium* [warm room, E], and *caldarium* [hot room, F] all had barrel-vaulted ceilings, while the *frigidarium* [cold room, G] had what may be the earliest surviving concrete dome in Italy, its *oculus* closed with a bronze disk which could be raised or lowered to regulate the temperature. In Vitruvius' chapter on baths (5.10) he mentions this device as appropriate for a *Laconicum*, or sweating room – a kind of Turkish Bath, which he says should be placed next to the *tepidarium*. Archaeologists therefore believe that this may have been the original function of what later became the *frigidarium* of the Stabian Baths.

After this 2nd century BC development, the only major addition to the Stabian Baths came in the reign of Augustus, when the western side of the site was remodelled to accommodate a *natatio* [swimming bath, H]. The irregular lay-out of the Stabian Baths continued to recall their early origin and long period of development, but they contained all the essential elements of the great imperial *thermae* which evolved in Rome over the next hundred years.

A second set of public baths, the Forum Baths, was built at Pompeii in about 80 BC and a third, the Central Baths, was under construction at the time of the eruption; in addition, some of the private houses had baths which the owners made available for public use on a commercial basis. Even so, the increasing importance of baths in city life during the empire is revealed by the contrast between this comparative scarcity and the 12 public baths recorded in the 3rd century AD at Timgad, which had a population only perhaps half as large again as Pompeii. In Rome itself, a 4th century AD inventory of the buildings in the city lists 856 *balnea*, private baths, and 11 *thermae*.

Rome: the Baths of Caracalla

The culmination of the series of great public baths came with the Baths of Caracalla, completed in AD 216. When compared to the Stabian Baths, two features of these are immediately apparent. The first is their sheer size: the main block (fig. 4.15) is almost ten times as big as the entire

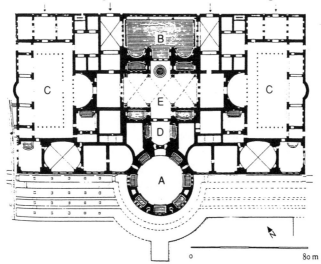

Fig. 4.15 Rome, Baths of Caracalla, plan

site of the Stabian Baths and it stands in an enclosure which is more than four times larger again, measuring over 400m. by over 300m. Secondly, there are in fact two sets of baths symmetrically arranged either side of the short axis and sharing the central elements from *caldarium* [A] to *natatio* [B].

Four doors on the north-east side gave entrance to the main block, the outer pair leading to the twin *palaestrae* [C] and the inner ones, either side of the *natatio*, to the main suite of baths. From these the main route led through to the south-west side, where – in accordance with Vitruvius' recommendation (5.10.1) – the hot rooms were arranged to catch the afternoon sun. In the centre of this side, and entered only through one small door on each side, so that the heat would not escape, the huge circular *caldarium* projected boldly. Its floor area was almost as large as that of the Pantheon and its dome rose considerably higher. As in the Pantheon, the drum wall was not equally thick all round and the weight of the dome was carried on eight piers. From the innermost of the recesses between these, two small doors provided a way through to the *tepidarium* [D], *frigidarium* [E] and *natatio*, and in the other seven stood hot plunge baths. Higher up in the drum eight large windows flooded the interior with light.

The *frigidarium* itself stood at the centre of the block, at the point where the long and short axes crossed. In basic design – three cross-vaults rising from eight piers – it resembled the Basilica Nova, but its position, surrounded by other rooms, shows why lighting could only be at clerestory level. As in the *caldarium*, the plunge baths were placed between the piers and the grand central space was reserved for socialising. To either side bathers could look through a screen of columns to lower, darker rooms and beyond them to the light unroofed space of the two *palaestrae*. Shallow apses in the central room at the far side of each *palaestra* emphasised the line of the cross axis and so helped the visitor to find his bearings in this huge complex.

The *natatio* was also open to the sky, though the high wall surrounding it must have given it a feeling of enclosure – another of the unroofed rooms of which the Romans were so fond. At either side screens of columns led through to the vaulted entrance rooms; the entrance from the *frigidarium* was flanked by two apses marked off by large granite columns, and the opposite wall had a two-storeyed facade of niches and columns rather like the *scaenae frons* of a theatre.

The huge enclosure in which this block stood was laid out with gardens, walks, fountains and statues and surrounded with a variety of buildings, recesses and colonnades. Along the middle of the south-west side was a running track with tiered seating for the spectators and above this were the cisterns which held the water supply for the baths, drawn direct from the Aqua Marcia. Elsewhere were lecture rooms and sheltered spaces for informal meetings and two libraries, one for works in Greek, the other for Latin.

The Baths of Caracalla are a masterpiece of the central tradition of Roman architecture, the development of a new material (concrete) and a new structural principle (the arch) and the exploitation of the possibilities offered by their combination (see Appendix). Their design satisfies the criteria both of functional efficiency and of aesthetic appeal, and comparison with the Pantheon demonstrates the advance in technical and artistic confidence Roman architects had made over the intervening ninety years. It is reckoned that some 1,600 people could use the Baths of Caracalla at any one time. In the central block alone, they would have expected to find lavishly decorated rooms of different temperatures, exercise areas and spaces for socialising, but they may sometimes have forgotten that these public rooms required a reliable water supply, furnaces, water pipes, raised floors and ducting for the circulation of warm air, and that all these needed regular maintenance. The clarity of the basic ground plan shows how well the architects understood these requirements, but they were not only interested in functionalism. The rooms show an exhilarating variety of shapes and sizes and are splendidly decorated, with mosaic floors, sumptuous use of coloured marble and granite for columns and wall panels, and coffered ceilings. Nor were the baths reserved for the rich and powerful: they were open, without charge, to all free inhabitants of Rome. And they were appreciated, for as an epitaph records – perhaps rather ironically – 'Hot baths, wine and sex ruin our health, but they make life worth living'.

Chapter 5
Private Housing

Two cities stand out for the contribution they make to the study of domestic architecture. Pompeii, together with its smaller neighbour Herculaneum, provides our best evidence for the *domus*, the individual family house owned by the more prosperous classes, while for the *insula*, the apartment block housing a number of tenants, we can turn to Ostia. Yet before starting to consider these two types of housing, it is important to emphasise that the differences between them are not just a matter of geography or social class but also of date. The eruption of Vesuvius put a sudden end to the life of Pompeii and Herculaneum in AD 79, whereas almost all the houses we can study at Ostia date from after AD 100.

(a) Pompeii and Herculaneum: the domus

The typical domus (fig. 5.1) was a single storey building formally

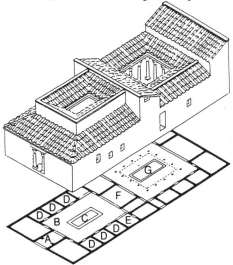

Fig. 5.1 Typical domus, axonometric view & plan

planned around two unroofed spaces, the atrium in the part nearer the street and the peristyle further back. The outside walls were largely blank, with few windows, and like many houses even nowadays in the Mediterranean area and the Near East the domus turned away from the heat and noise of the outside world to provide an oasis of calm within.

Through the main entrance and the relatively ill-lit *fauces* [A], you would enter the atrium itself [B], whose formal design, impressive size and rich decoration marked it out as the heart of the domus. Its most striking feature was the opening in the roof, the *compluvium*, which provided light and air for the atrium and from which rain water fell into the *impluvium* [C], the shallow pool in the centre of the floor immediately below. (In many houses the water was then stored in a cistern underneath, but sometimes there was no cistern and the water was taken off in pipes either to the garden or to the streets outside.) On either side of the atrium two or three large doors led into simply furnished bedrooms [D] lit, if at all, only by tiny windows set high up in the outside walls or above the door from the atrium. The space immediately around the *impluvium* was covered by the wide overhang of the roof, supported on huge wooden beams and providing protection from both winter storms and summer heat. Beyond the *impluvium*, the atrium was open across the full width of the house, extending to recesses on either side [E] which the Romans called 'wings' (*alae*). This additional space had the effect of drawing attention to the broad facade of the rooms which faced the visitor as he entered the atrium. In the centre of these, immediately opposite the *fauces*, was the *tablinum* [F]. It was often flanked by pilasters and approached by a step up from the atrium – features which emphasised its status as the most important room in the house – and usually stood open to the peristyle garden beyond, but could be shut off when necessary by a wooden screen or heavy curtains. A dining room (*triclinium*) often stood to one side of the *tablinum*.

The second main source of light for the domus was the peristyle [G], an open space surrounded by a colonnade and usually containing a small formal garden. Superficially similar to the atrium, it yet had a much lighter and less enclosed feel to it and the arrangement of rooms in this part of the house was less rigidly formal than in the atrium. There would often be a summer *triclinium*, set to catch the afternoon sun, and one or more *exedrae*, recesses where the family could sit and relax, enjoying the play of water from the fountains in the garden and the gleam of marble or bronze statuary among the plants. Some of the service rooms – kitchen, bathroom, latrine, servants' quarters – were also often found along one side of the peristyle.

Vitruvius distinguishes (6.5.1) between the parts of the house which were for the use of the owner and his family and for invited guests and those which were open to the public. The most important of the latter was the atrium itself, for this was the setting for the *salutatio*, one of the most significant rituals of Roman social life, when the owner of the house received morning greetings from his *clientes*, dealt with the requests they brought him, and indicated the kind of support he required from them. Another was the *tablinum*, which served as a kind of headquarters office for the owner's commercial and political activities and where the strongbox containing important documents was kept. Vitruvius goes on to explain that poorer people do not need splendid atria and tablina, since they fulfil their social obligations by visiting the houses of more important citizens rather than by having others come to them, and his comment demonstrates how firmly the design of the domus is based upon social function. For the other parts of the domus – dining rooms and bedrooms, for example – the visitor required an invitation from the owner.

Interior Decoration

The furnishing and decoration of these houses showed a surprising mixture of richness and simplicity. By modern standards there was relatively little furniture, but the craftsmanship shown in the inlaid wood of beds and couches or the bronze of tables and candelabra was often of a very high standard. By contrast, mosaic floors and wall paintings were common. The former ranged from the simplest black and white geometrical patterns to the elaborate full-colour representation of Alexander the Great at the Battle of the Issus which occupied the entire floor (3.2m. x 5.5m.) of an exedra in the peristyle of the House of the Faun (fig. 5.3 D). Wall paintings too varied considerably in style as fashions succeeded each other. The earliest houses, like the House of Sallust, had panels painted in plain colours to imitate marble veneer; later, mythological scenes or architectural fantasies became popular, or the walls were painted with coastal scenes and landscapes, so that a feeling of the fresh countryside was brought into the enclosed world of the domus. Often too there were statues, in bronze and marble, both in the interior of the house and in the garden.

Origin of the Atrium

In practice, of course, none of the actual houses in Pompeii or Herculaneum conforms exactly to the typical pattern. In particular, there is a clear line of development over time from houses where the atrium is the most important feature to those where it has become little more than an entrance hall.

The origin of the atrium – and what seems the strange idea of having a hole in your roof – is still not settled. One suggestion is that to start with it was roofed right over, and that the *compluvium* opening was a response to the need for light as houses increased in size. It is true that Vitruvius refers to roofed atria (6.3.2) as suitable for smaller houses, and the houses of the poorer classes in Pompeii and Herculaneum are often loosely arranged around a roofed central space, but although this sometimes has a touch of formality, it is often little more than a broad central corridor. Others argue that the atrium started as an open yard surrounded by separate buildings with overhanging roofs, and that it was the typically Italian liking for a sense of enclosure which led to its reduction in size and its treatment as an interior space. Houses from about the middle of the 3rd century BC at Cosa have an interior courtyard extending across the full width, like the *alae* of the domus, and with the main rooms facing across this towards the entrance. These may represent a kind of mid-point in the process of development from courtyard to atrium.

The House of Sallust

One of the clearest examples of an atrium house at Pompeii is the House of Sallust (fig. 5.2). In its original form, in the early to mid 3rd century BC, this had no peristyle and consisted only of the atrium and its associated rooms, set within a large walled garden and fronted by three

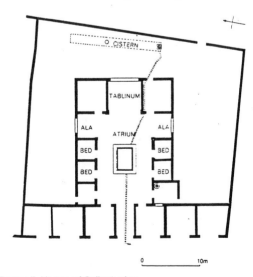

Fig. 5.2 Pompeii, House of Sallust, plan

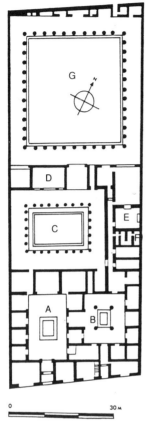

0   30 M

Fig. 5.3 Pompeii, House of the Faun, plan

symmetrically planned shops either side of the entrance. Although the site is irregular, the house itself is almost completely symmetrical about the axis from entrance to tablinum. Its formality seems to express an age when the power of authority figures at every level of society from family to state was hardly questioned.

The House of the Faun

In the course of the 2nd century the peristyle also began to come into fashion, a further example of the increasing Greek influence during this period that we have already seen when considering temple architecture. The introduction of a second centre for the house perhaps suggests that the rituals of social life were becoming more complex and that the owner found it useful to be able to discriminate yet more precisely between visitors of different rank.

The House of the Faun (fig. 5.3), the largest and one of the most coherently planned of all Pompeian houses, has a particularly complex version of the combination of atrium and peristyle. It actually has two atria: the western one [A], its roof carried on beams in the traditional style Vitruvius calls Tuscan, was for the formal business of the head of the household; the one to the east [B], which already has something of the feel of a peristyle since its roof is supported by columns, may have been for the more private side of family life. Behind them, is the first of the two peristyles [C], probably built around 125 BC. Its planning shows something of a compromise between fashion and the traditional claims of symmetry, for the positioning of its main room, the exedra with the Alexander mosaic [D], on the axis of the Tuscan atrium goes some way to concealing the fact that, in relation to the house as a whole, this peristyle is unsymmetrically placed. To the east of this peristyle were placed the kitchen [E] and the earliest example at Pompeii of a bath in a private house [F], while behind it a second peristyle [G] occupied the full width of the block.

Although the House of Sallust expanded to take up most of what had originally been garden, its impressive atrium remained relatively intact, while the House of the Faun was hardly changed at all, remaining a splendid example of a republican domus right up to the destruction of the city in AD 79. Naturally enough, however, most of the houses which we can see at Pompeii or Herculaneum illustrate the architectural styles of the cities' final years. They show a continuing trend towards looser, more varied, plans and a continuing decline in the importance of the atrium.

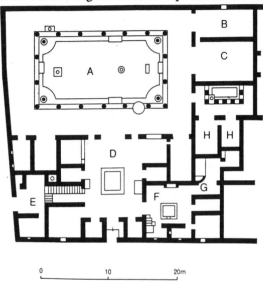

Fig. 5.4 Pompeii, House of the Vettii, plan

The House of the Vettii

One of the most informative houses of this period, since it was almost entirely built between the earthquake which devastated Pompeii in AD 62 and the eruption of Vesuvius seventeen years later, is the House of the Vettii (fig. 5.4). Here the focus of the architect's plan is the peristyle [A] or, more precisely, the garden at its centre, with its attractive combination of plants, marble statuary and cool fountains. The unusually wide colonnade around the garden provided a kind of outdoor sitting room and the main rooms opened off it. All but one of these were sumptuously decorated with wall paintings in the latest style. (The narrow room in the northwest corner [B] was still unfinished at the time of the eruption.) The large dining room [C], for example, commanding a view down the full length of the garden from the north-west end, was decorated with panels of red separated by bands of black; some of these panels carried scenes from Greek mythology, while the main ones once held paintings on wood, which were presumably removed immediately after the eruption; beneath the panels was a frieze of little Cupids playing at various tasks like winemaking or chariot racing.

The house did have a more or less symmetrical atrium [D], but in the absence of a tablinum it had lost its original social function and served mainly as an entrance hall, linking the different sections of the house. Straight ahead, it led into the peristyle; to the south-east, a corridor ran through to the stable yard [E] and to the latrine, placed conveniently close to the sewer beneath the street outside; to the north-east, one could enter a second atrium [F], which led in turn to the kitchen courtyard [G] and on to a secluded pair of rooms [H], often described as the Women's Quarters but more probably a further reception room with a bedroom beside it, which faced on to a small colonnaded garden; and from there one could return to the peristyle. The different parts of the house, each with its own function, are kept separate but passage between them is fluid. The plan is much looser than was the case in earlier houses but its aim was still to enable the owners to make a public display of their wealth and status.

Herculaneum: The House of the Mosaic Atrium and the House of the Stags

The same tendency can be seen at Herculaneum. Two adjacent houses, the House of the Mosaic Atrium and the House of the Stags (fig. 5.5), were built out over the city walls shortly before AD 79. Both have an atrium

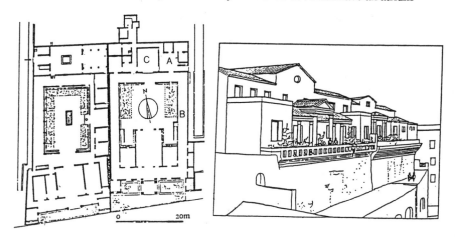

Fig. 5.5 Herculaneum, House of the Mosaic Atrium & House of the Stags

but its decline in status is clear. In the House of the Stags, indeed, it has become no more than an awkwardly shaped entrance hall [A], entirely roofed over, and without tablinum or anything else to give it a sense of direction. The peristyle [B] surrounding the garden is also very different from the usual colonnade; it is an enclosed corridor, looking out on to the garden only through large windows pierced in its walls. Yet the house is still symmetrically planned, about the long axis from the inner triclinium [C] to the pavilion [D] at the centre of the terrace, with its wide views out over the Bay of Naples to Capri and the mountains of the Sorrento peninsula.

Architecture and Social Change

These changes in architectural fashion seem to have been accompanied by changes in the social composition of the population of Pompeii and Herculaneum. Some of the leading families ceased to use their town houses, preferring to move out to villas in the surrounding countryside, and the increasing popularity of upper storeys and the tendency for single family houses to pass into multiple occupation suggest that the population may have been growing.

The earliest examples of upper storeys occur in the 2nd century BC, when there was something of a fashion for building dining rooms at first floor level, but most of them date from after about 50 BC. In a late house – the House of the Vettii, for example, (fig. 5.4) where stairs can be seen in the corridor leading to the stable yard and in a corner of the smaller atrium – they may have been an integral part of the architect's original plan, but in most cases they were additions to existing buildings and so of light construction, often just wattle and daub.

The six shops flanking the entrance to the House of Sallust (fig. 5.2) show that even as early as the 3rd century BC the most aristocratic residents might have less distinguished neighbours. The ground floors of these establishments would have been where the business was carried on, while a kind of wooden gallery towards the back provided living space for the shopkeeper and his family. The number of shops and workshops like this increased and they sometimes expanded back into what had once been the residential part of a house to acquire more room for their commercial activities.

In the 1st century AD we also find that some of the houses were split up into separate apartments which the owners rented out to tenants. A notice painted on the wall outside the Villa of Julia Felix, a large house with extensive grounds, situated towards the eastern end of the

Pompeii, illustrates the situation. It records that the property was to let in three sections: the owner's residential quarters, including living rooms, peristyle and garden; a suite of baths rented out for public use; an inn, a shop and some apartments with separate front doors.

Pompeii: The House of the Menander and its Block

Accounts of Pompeii naturally tend to focus on the more splendid houses and to treat them as individual examples of the development of the domus rather than as parts of an urban fabric which also included the houses, shops and workshops of the poorer classes. They also give greater attention to the situation in the final years, since this is the period when there is most evidence, than to the processes of change which led up to that situation. The detailed work done by a team of British archaeologists on a complete block of houses (figs 3.7 K; 5.6) between 1978 and 1986 helps to provide a more balanced account.

    The main house in the block, the House of the Menander [A] was one of the most impressive in Pompeii and in its final form covered more than half the block. The residential quarters were based round the standard atrium and peristyle, but it also had a private bath suite, kitchen and vegetable garden [B] to the west of the peristyle, a large banqueting hall to its east [C], and in the south-east corner a stable yard [D] – with

Fig. 5.6 Pompeii, House of the Menander, plan of block

a gate wide enough to admit farm carts – and servants' quarters. In the south-west corner, the House of the Lovers [E] also had both atrium and peristyle, the latter almost unique in Pompeii in having two storeys. Both these houses certainly belonged to the wealthier classes, but the block also contained some poorer dwellings occupied by residents of much lower status. The two houses in the north-west corner [F & G] are still fairly regular and have at least an atrium, though no peristyle. The House of the Cabinet Maker [F] contained wood-working tools and other indications of its owner's craft, while the corner house [G] may have been occupied by a weaver, since a number of loom weights were found there. Three smaller houses in the north-east corner present a thoroughly irregular and confused jig-saw puzzle of boundary walls. Finally, the small establishment in the south-east corner [H] was a cafe-bar; the workshop [I] between the House of the Menander and the House of the Cabinet Maker seems to have been occupied by a fuller; and the erotic graffiti on the stairs beside its entrance suggest that they led up to a brothel on the first floor. The social composition of the block was certainly mixed.

The history of how the block developed also reveals a number of interesting points. Construction did not begin until shortly before 200 BC and parts of the block remained unoccupied until about AD 50. Property boundaries always seem to have been fluid. The House of the Menander was always the most important building, starting as a symmetrical atrium house like the House of Sallust and expanding to absorb vacant space or take over rooms that had previously belonged to other houses. The House of the Lovers was built over an earlier property entered from the south, while the three houses in the north-east corner occupied a space previously shared between only two.

Changes in property use were also common. When the north-east corner house was stepped back during the reign of Augustus to make room for a street-corner fountain, its owner turned his front room into a cafe-bar, but by AD 79 it had reverted to residential use. The fullery and brothel and the cafe-bar carved out of the stables in the south-east corner all date from after the earthquake of AD 62. The earliest upper storeys were built about 50 BC but they became more common from the end of the 1st century BC, and by AD 79 almost every property in the block had at least a partial upper floor. These discoveries provide pointers to trends that may also have applied in other parts of Pompeii, and indeed in Herculaneum and other cities of Italy.

(B) Ostia: the insula

Tenement Buildings in Rome

> An ox climbed up to the third storey of a building near the cattle
> market in Rome and then, terrified by the din the tenants raised,
> hurled itself to the ground. (Livy, 21.62)

Livy records this little incident as one of the portents sent by the gods in
the winter of 218/7 BC to warn the Romans that they would face further
disasters in their war against the Carthaginians. We may not believe the
divine message, but the story is important as evidence that buildings
several storeys high were to be found in Rome before the end of the 3rd
century BC. At least parts of the city must already have been crowded.

From other sources too we know that at this period Rome was an
ill-planned city with a higgledy-piggledy warren of narrow streets, the
result of hasty rebuilding after its destruction by the Gauls in 390 BC.
Small wonder, then, that it was so liable to fire.

The Great Fire of Rome

The most destructive of these fires was the terrible one in AD 64, in the
reign of Nero. Three of the fourteen regions of the city were totally
destroyed and seven others were badly affected. Unkind rumour has it
that Nero fiddled while Rome burned: in fact, he took energetic steps to
deal with the immediate problems and produced an intelligent set of
regulations to govern the eventual reconstruction programme. To ensure
that those who had lost their houses did not starve and had somewhere
to live, he reduced the price of corn and had temporary shelters erected
in various of the city's open spaces, including his own gardens. The ships
which brought corn up the Tiber were not allowed to return downstream
empty but had to take on a cargo of rubble from the collapsed buildings
and land it at Ostia to be dumped in the marshes there. Rewards were
promised to owners who rebuilt their properties within a specified time.
For the future, streets were to have a minimum width and the height of
buildings was restricted. (This was probably a re-enactment of the
Augustan limit of 70 Roman feet. Trajan later reduced it to 60 feet.) Each
apartment block was to be surrounded by its own wall – i.e. adjacent
blocks should not share a party wall, since this would make it easier for
fire to pass from one to the other – and to have a courtyard containing a
supply of water. Up to a certain height, wooden beams were banned and

buildings were to be made of stone from Gabii or Alba, since this was reckoned fire-resistant.

It is impossible to be sure that these regulations were always observed – quite probably not – but the city which arose after the fire was certainly very different from its predecessor. Tacitus comments that the new regulations were approved for their utility and also made the city more beautiful, though he adds that some people felt that the winding streets of the old city and the higher buildings had protected them better from the heat of the sun (*Annals*, 15.43). The reconstruction of the city probably encouraged the tendency away from the single-storey domus towards the insula or apartment block. The 4th century AD inventory of the buildings in Rome recorded 46,602 apartment blocks and only 1,790 individual houses. Yet none of these apartment blocks survives, and if we want to see what they looked like, we must visit Ostia.

The Development of Ostia

At the beginning of AD 79 the residential areas of Ostia would have resembled those which were so soon to be destroyed – and so preserved – in Pompeii and Herculaneum. In both, the standard form of housing was still the domus, but the next fifty years were a period of rapid change, and by the middle of the 2nd century AD Ostia was a city of apartment blocks.

The reason for this change was a huge increase in population caused by the development of Ostia as the main port for Rome, and particularly as the main centre for the import of corn to feed the population of the capital. (Fig. 3.3 G shows some of the granaries.) Its proximity to Rome and the fact that goods could be taken on by river (land transport was much more expensive) gave it two great advantages, but as trade increased the harbour became too small, and matters were made worse by silting at the mouth of the Tiber. To try to improve the situation, the Emperor Claudius built a new harbour about 4 km. north of the river mouth, protecting it by huge moles built out from the land on either side and linking it to the Tiber by canal. This provided useful extra space but proved too exposed – in AD 62 two hundred ships were destroyed by storm inside the harbour – and so the Emperor Trajan added an inner harbour, which provided safe mooring for over a hundred ships. Although a new settlement, Portus, grew up around Trajan's harbour, Ostia remained the centre for the whole complex and was at its busiest and most prosperous during the 2nd century AD. A measure of the population growth that accompanied these developments is provided by comparing the density of population in Ostia with that in Pompeii. The area enclosed by the walls was the same in each city, about 65 hectares, but whereas the population of Pompeii in AD 79 was probably only about 10,000, at Ostia it rose to about 50,000 in the 2nd century AD.

The Insula

In a situation like this, one advantage of the insula is obvious: it can house a large number of people in a relatively small area. Another comes from its method of construction and the materials used. Walls of brick-faced concrete, though strong and having good powers of resistance to fire, can be built quickly without the need to call on expensive craft skills, and the cost of the materials themselves and of transporting them to the site is relatively cheap.

The height of insulae varied, usually between three and five storeys. In a few parts of Ostia walls still stand to the foot of the third storey, but the main evidence for the height of a building comes from the thickness of its ground floor walls: in general, a wall 60cm. thick suggests a building of three storeys, while one of five storeys usually has walls nearly a metre thick. The average height of each storey at Ostia was about 3.5m., though ground floors might reach almost four metres, so a building of five storeys could just be accommodated within Trajan's limit of 60 Roman feet (about 17.75m.), especially if the top storey was rather lower. The other building regulations introduced in Rome by Nero after the great fire seem also to have been observed in Ostia. Buildings are usually enclosed by their own walls and the use of wood for structural purposes was rare, at least in the lower storeys.

The bare brick, red or yellowish in colour and set in narrow horizontal bands (*opus testaceum*), gave a uniform appearance to the exterior walls. Variety and a sense of rhythm were provided by windows – sometimes containing coarse glass, sometimes merely shuttered – and in some cases by balconies or by the wide entrances of shops at ground level. The balconies are not always accessible from the apartments behind them and they seem rather to have been built as an amenity for the town in general, to shelter the people using the streets. The shops are often roofed with a concrete barrel vault, which must have improved the stability of the whole building and provided a strong foundation for the residential storeys above. The small square windows just above the entrance provided light for the cramped living quarters of the shopkeeper and his family.

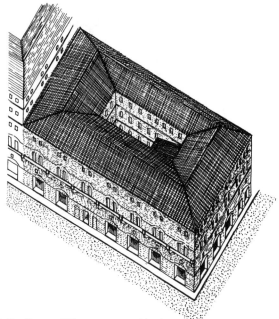

Fig. 5.7 Ostia, House of Diana, axonometric view

The House of Diana

The House of Diana (figs 3.3F, 5.7) illustrates many of these points. Like many other insulae in Ostia, it is a rectangular block arranged around an inner courtyard. This had little in common with the majestic atria or elegant peristyles of the Pompeian domus and must often have seemed a dark and cheerless space. Its main functions were to provide light for rooms without external windows and to house the water supply for the entire block. Only in some of the more luxurious apartment blocks did the courtyard have much aesthetic appeal; in the House of the Charioteers, for example, it is surrounded at ground level by an open arcade. Other blocks, such as the Cassette-tipo, have no courtyard but extend along the street like a terrace.

Internal Lay-out: the Cassette-tipo

There was always more variety to the internal lay-out of insulae than in the fairly regular plan of the domus, but the Cassette-tipo (fig. 5.8, see next page) exhibit one fairly common pattern. There were no shops in this block and the apartment shown was on the ground floor. The

Scale 1:150.

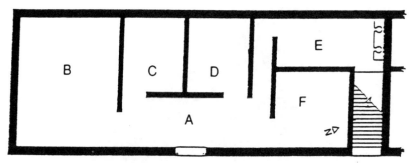

Fig. 5.8 Ostia, Cassette-tipo, plan

entrance, from the street on the east side, led direct into the *medianum* [A], the central space around which the other rooms were arranged. These included a fairly large living room[B], two bedrooms [C and D], a latrine [E], and a room which may have served as a kitchen [F]. There were windows along the east side and at the south end but none on the west, except perhaps for a small vent in the latrine. The apartment above and the corresponding pair at the north end would have had a similar lay-out.

This was one of the earliest blocks in Ostia, dating from about AD 100, and was probably only two storeys high. It did not have piped water, was not well built, and the two-seater latrine has been taken to suggest that it was overcrowded (though it may only indicate that the boundary between public and private acts was not the same in Roman society as in our own). Despite this, there were black and white mosaics on the floors of all the rooms except the latrine and the walls were stuccoed and painted. The residents of this block were probably quite poor, but many insulae had tenants from all social classes. In these, the wealthiest generally lived on the ground floor, if there were no shops, or immediately above that, while the poorest would be in the smaller apartments at the very top.

An additional advantage of the basic insula plan was that with only quite minor changes it could be used for different types of building. Two buildings from the middle of the 2nd century AD illustrate this. The Headquarters of the Fire Brigade (fig. 5.9 A, see next page) and a large warehouse for corn (fig. 5.9 B) are both built of brick-faced concrete and organised around an inner courtyard.

The Decline of Ostia

Ostia's period of prosperity as a working town was quite short, little more than 150 years, and from about AD 250 Portus gained in importance and

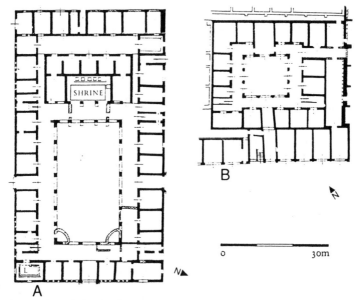

Fig. 5.9 Ostia, HQ of Vigiles & warehouse, plan

the population of Ostia began to fall. When a large bakery with residential accommodation on the upper floors burnt down shortly after AD 250 it was not rebuilt, and routine repair work to the warehouses seems almost to have ceased before the end of the century. However, the decline in population and the fall in the value of land which accompanied it had one interesting result. The individual house came back into fashion, and in the 4th century AD Ostia became a pleasant residential town with baths, theatre, nymphaeum, and all the other amenities of urban life.

But even this did not last long. The prosperity of Ostia always depended upon that of Rome, and with the foundation of a new capital of the empire at Constantinople in AD 330, with general insecurity reducing trade between different parts of the empire, and with plague affecting its population, Rome itself now began to decline. In the late 5th century AD the aqueduct supplying Ostia fell out of use – it was probably too expensive to maintain any longer – and the residents were forced to rely once again on digging wells. By the 6th century AD, few inhabitants remained. As time passed, the 'new' harbours silted up, the coastline shifted, and the drainage channels ceased to function. By the Middle Ages, the site of Ostia was surrounded by extensive swamps and the whole area was subject to malaria.

Intermittent campaigns of excavation took place in the 19th century, a matter at first mainly of hunting for sculpture and inscriptions, but systematic work designed to reveal the appearance and life of the city as a whole did not start until the early years of the 20th century.

The Reputation of the Insula: Juvenal

Without these excavations, we should still not know what an insula looked like and should still have to piece together our picture from references in Latin literature. The most often quoted of these writers is the satirist Juvenal who wrote early in the 2nd century AD, some fifty to sixty years after the redevelopment of Rome following the great fire. In *Satire 3*, Juvenal attacked the corruption and misery of life in Rome:

> Most of the city we live in is shored up by flimsy props. That's how the landlord stops it collapsing, papering over the gaping cracks and telling us to go to sleep, not to worry – though the house is already swaying and about to fall.

He also refers to the risk of fire, describing the fate of the poor tenant on the top floor, who is always the last to hear the alarm and scarcely has time to escape with his life:

> Codrus had nothing...yet the poor fellow lost all the nothing he had. (Juvenal, 3.193-6, 208-9)

For many centuries this highly critical view of Rome as a city of collapsing houses and constant fires dominated people's ideas about the insula. Now that we also have the archaeological evidence from Ostia, we ought to ask how accurate Juvenal's account is or whether he exaggerated, even perhaps distorted, the facts in order to make his satirical point.

Were the insulae of Ostia liable to sudden collapse? They seem solid and well built on the whole, and 'there are few signs of major reconstruction or restoration on the ground floors dictated by the need to strengthen the building.' (Russell Meiggs, *Roman Ostia*, p. 250.) How frequent were fires? In the *Fasti* (official calendar) for Ostia we read that on 1st January AD 115, 'a fire broke out in the town and several properties were burnt.'

Oil lamps, braziers, and the practice of cooking in an enclosed space were constant hazards, while the existence of a regular fire brigade in Ostia and the harsh penalties prescribed under the law – careless use of fires in an insula could be punished by birching or flogging (*Digest*, 1.15.3.4) – suggest that the authorities took the risk of fire seriously. Yet brick-faced concrete has good powers of resistance to fire, and the archaeological record provides no evidence of major fires in Ostia. At the end of *Satire* 1, Juvenal explains that he will not criticise the living but will pick his targets from among those whose tombs already line the roads into Rome. In a rather similar way, the housing standards he criticises may not be those of his own day but those of pre-Neronian Rome, and his entertaining attack may owe more to literary tradition than to careful observation. Certainly, his criticisms closely echo those which Strabo expressed about the city in the reign of Augustus (5.3.7).

A recent writer on Ostia reaches a conclusion very different from Juvenal's; he writes of:

> highly civilized apartment houses, spacious and full of air and light, reaching up three, four, or five storeys, with a sophisticated utilization of space that is only matched in modern times (Gustav Hermansen, *Ostia*, p. 10).

Chapter 6
Aftermath

Survival

Two events in the 5th century AD are often taken to mark the end of the Roman Empire in the West: the capture of Rome by the Visigothic leader, Alaric, in 410 and the deposition of the last emperor, Romulus Augustulus, in 476. (In the East, one could reasonably argue that the Roman Empire continued until 1453, when the Turks captured Constantinople.) Yet historical change is seldom either as sudden or as complete as these precise dates suggest. The Empire had changed greatly even before 410 – its official religion, for example, had been Christian for about a hundred years and its capital had been Constantinople, not Rome – and much survived even after 476. This was notably true in the field of architecture and town planning.

Despite warfare and invasion, most of the cities of Italy which had flourished during the Empire continued to function in the Middle Ages. Security was obviously a prime consideration, and walls and gates were kept in good repair. Within them, there is evidence that the habit, and indeed the spirit, of urban living were kept up by the municipal authorities. The town plans of such modern cities as Verona, Piacenza and Pavia show that their original Roman grids have remained in use without significant interruption. In several cities too, the site of the Roman forum continued as an open square, often serving as a market place for the mediaeval city. A poem of about AD 800 describes Verona as having 'a broad, spacious forum paved with stone and with a large arch at each corner'.

Individual buildings were also well preserved, particularly when their original function was still important or they could be adapted for fresh use. The municipal granaries at Brescia remained in use throughout the Middle Ages, while those at Arezzo had been converted into housing by 876. Particularly strong and solid buildings, whatever their original purpose, made good fortresses. In Rome alone, the Arches of Titus and Constantine, the Theatre of Marcellus, and the Colosseum were all occupied by various of the noble families whose feuds were such a feature of Roman history in the Middle Ages, and the Mausoleum of Hadrian, standing guard over the route across the Tiber to the Vatican, served the same purpose for the popes.

A particular type of re-use is the conversion of Roman buildings into Christian churches. At first it was mainly secular buildings which were treated in this way: the temples were too tainted by their pagan associations. A round building next to the Basilica Nova in the Forum became the church of Saints Cosmas and Damian in 526-30; towards the end of the 11th century the Senate House took on a new life as the church of St Hadrian; as late as 1559 Michelangelo converted the frigidarium of the Baths of Diocletian into the church of Santa Maria degli Angeli. The case of the Pantheon has already been described in Chapter 1. Apart from this, the earliest conversion from temple to church was probably that of the Temple of Portunus in the Forum Boarium (Cattle Market) in about 872-6.

Yet the prestige of the Christian Church required more than just recycled pagan buildings; once recognised as the official religion it had also to build from scratch on a scale large enough and in a style rich enough to justify its new status. From early in the 4th century architects met this requirement by adapting existing designs, in particular by basing the design of their major churches on that of the traditional basilica. The earliest such church, St John Lateran (fig. 6.1) built in Rome about AD 320, provides a good example. Like the Basilica Nova, completed only a few years earlier, it was built of brick-faced concrete and its interior was sumptuously decorated with coloured marbles, mosaics and gilding, but in plan and in the use of a ridge roof rather than vaulting it more

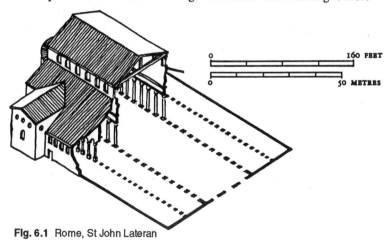

0   160 FEET

0   50 METRES

Fig. 6.1 Rome, St John Lateran

Fig. 6.2 Arles, Amphitheatre in 18th century

closely resembled the Basilica Ulpia in Trajan's Forum, or the basilica which Septimius Severus built at Leptis Magna. This pattern, longitudinal with the altar providing a point of focus at one end, became the standard one for churches throughout western Europe and its influence can be seen to the present day.

Outside Italy, and particularly further out towards the fringes of the empire, survivals become less common. The Rhône valley is still rich in Roman buildings and shows some of the same features as Italy. The amphitheatre at Arles became a fortified residential quarter in the Middle Ages, containing a church and over two hundred houses (fig. 6.2), while at Orange the theatre and triumphal arch were incorporated in the city fortifications. The Maison Carrée at Nîmes owes its survival in such excellent condition to its continued use for a variety of purposes: assembly hall, private house, stable, church, granary, town hall; it even acquired a second life in the New World by inspiring Thomas Jefferson's 1785 design for the State House at Richmond, Virginia (fig. 6.3). But in this part of France, as in Italy, city life continued to function.

Fig. 6.3 Richmond, Virginia, State House

Further north, the urban population declined steeply towards the end of the Roman Empire and in the early Middle Ages, and the area enclosed within the Roman walls was often too large for the few remaining inhabitants. At Autun, two separate fortified settlements grew up within the circuit of the Roman walls – and some cities, such as Silchester and Wroxeter, were eventually abandoned. Where a city did continue to function, protection against attack was important and parts at least of the city walls often remained in use. In Britain, an almost complete circuit can be seen at the mini-city of Caerwent in South Wales and there are good stretches of Roman walling incorporated in the mediaeval fortifications of Lincoln and London. The drop in population is one reason why, even when a city remained an important centre of government, like Winchester, much of the Roman street pattern was lost. Another is the fact that buildings were seldom entirely made of stone: very often they had footings of stone but above that were only of timber contruction and so were much more likely to collapse into ruin than the stone buildings of Italy or the south of France.

Revival

The Renaissance, the period of European cultural history characterised by a passionate interest in the 'rebirth' or rediscovery of the thought and art of ancient Greece and Rome, originated in Italy in the 14th century and gradually spread to the rest of Europe. Italian architects of the later Middle Ages were certainly familiar with the Roman buildings which survived to their day, and it is tempting to ask whether in this sphere at least there was any need for a period of rediscovery. What distinguishes the architects of the Renaissance is that they were not satisfied with this purely practical knowledge but sought to underpin it with a theoretical understanding of architecture and its role which could be applied to everything they designed.

Manuscripts of Vitruvius were known in the Middle Ages, but his *de Architectura* became particularly influential once it was recognised in the early 15th century as the only work on architecture to survive from Roman times. The first printed edition appeared in Rome in 1486, an edition with illustrations in 1511, and further editions and translations throughout the 16th and 17th centuries. His work also inspired Renaissance architects and scholars to write their own treatises.

The first of these, Alberti's *Art of Building* of 1452, defined beauty in architecture as a kind of harmony and correct proportion of all the parts – an echo perhaps of Vitruvius' comment on the importance of symmetry (1.2.4) but also the statement of a principle that was to be of central importance for the artists and architects of the Renaissance; he also followed Vitruvius in insisting that the architect should be a man of wide general education and experience. (This claim may also owe something to Alberti's own reputation as one of the most versatile men of his age – mathematician, musician, painter, philosopher, poet, athlete as well as architect.) Alberti's church of St. Andrea at Mantua (1470) shows how he put theory into practice. Its facade (fig. 6.4) sets a Roman triumphal arch beneath a temple pediment, while internally the vault of the nave is buttressed by chapels set transversely to it in a manner reminiscent of the Basilica Nova.

Fig. 6.4 Mantua, St Andrea

Of the many important works of theory written in the next two hundred years the most influential was probably Palladio's *Four Books of Architecture*, published in 1615. Palladio was a practical architect as well as a scholar, and the variety of ways in which he made use of Roman precedents in his own work can be illustrated by two of his buildings. The Teatro Olimpico at Vicenza (1580) was intended to be an accurate reconstruction of the Roman theatre as described by Vitruvius (5.6) and was the fruit of a lifetime's study. It was the equivalent in

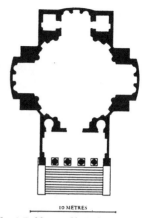

10 METRES

Fig. 6.5 Maser, Chapel

architecture of the attempts being made by literary scholars of the day to revive Greek and Roman drama. At about the same time Palladio built a chapel at Maser (fig. 6.5), just north of Vicenza. Like his earlier Villa Rotonda, it derives from the Pantheon but it is not just an academic copy. Palladio opened up the circular drum of the Pantheon into the more obviously Christian shape of a Greek cross, taking the elements he needed from antiquity and adapting them to a new purpose.

In Britain the first architect to show the influence of the Renaissance works of architectural theory and to build in Classical style was Inigo Jones, the 'Vitruvius of his age' as one of his pupils described him. His church of St Paul's, Covent Garden, London (fig. 6.6), built in

Fig. 6.6 London, St Paul's, Covent Garden

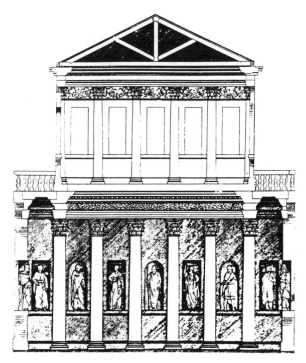

Fig. 6.7 Vitruvius' Egyptian Hall

1631, is based on Vitruvius' description of the Tuscan temple (4.7) and is perhaps the nearest thing in Britain to the Capitolium at Cosa.

Their main influence, however, came about a hundred years later in the artistic circle surrounding Lord Burlington, when the appeal of proportion and restraint seemed all the greater after the extravagance of the English Baroque. In 1730 Burlington himself published a set of drawings Palladio had made of the great imperial thermae of Rome. He also produced in his design for the Assembly Rooms at York (1732) a version of the 'Egyptian hall' Vitruvius had described (6.3.9) and for which Palladio had produced an illustration (fig. 6.7). Other members of the group also combined theory and practice. William Kent edited the *Drawings of Inigo Jones* (1727) and Colen Campbell published three volumes of engravings of British buildings showing Roman influence under the title *Vitruvius Britannicus* (1715-25). Campbell also built a version of Palladio's Villa Rotonda at Mereworth Castle (1725), and Lord Burlington took the same model for the villa he designed for his own use at Chiswick a year or so later.

The influence of Roman architecture continued and often displayed the same link between the study of antiquity and the practice of architects engaged in the day-to-day business of their profession. In 1753, for example, Robert Wood and James Dawkins published *The Ruins of Palmyra*; less than ten years later, Robert Adam made use of their engraving of a ceiling in the 1st century AD Temple of Bel for the dining room ceiling at Osterley House, Middlesex. In the interior lay-out of the country houses he designed Adam was influenced by the sequence of rooms of different shapes and sizes which he had observed in the Baths of Caracalla when studying in Rome. The same aspect of the Baths, as illustrated in an 1828 French publication, impressed H.L. Elmes when he produced the design which won the competition for St George's Hall, Liverpool in 1840.

Decline?

Yet the architectural context in which Elmes based his design on a feature from the Baths of Caracalla was very different from the one in which Adam had done so. Up to about 1750 the only past from which architects could borrow was that of Rome – described by Vitruvius, visible in the surviving monuments, studied and interpreted by architects like Alberti, Palladio and Inigo Jones. True, Vitruvius had made frequent reference to the Greeks, but their buildings were further afield and more difficult to visit. Around 1750 the situation began to change. Travellers on the Grand Tour extended their journeys to southern Italy and Sicily or to Greece itself and books with accurately measured drawings of Greek architecture began to appear. (Stuart and Revett's *Antiquities of Athens*, the most influential in this country, was published in 1762.) It became clear that there was not just one form of Classical architecture but that, although Greek and Roman architects made use of certain common motifs, notably the orders, their approaches to building were fundamentally different. Architects were faced with a choice.

How could they decide? For some, the greater antiquity of Greek architecture was significant: because it was older, it must somehow be truer and closer to nature. This was an important point at a time when the established order was coming under attack in so many fields – politics, literature, philosophy, music – and the claims of simplicity and nature were being set against it. In 1753, the Abbe Laugier had published his *Essay on Architecture*, in which he claimed that all subsequent architecture derived from the first ever attempt at building – a simple hut to provide shelter from the elements, constructed from tree trunks leaning against each other to make a kind of wigwam; the next step, he thought, came when the trunks were stood upright and linked by horizontal cross pieces. From this primitive post and lintel system (see Appendix) he could deduce the whole development of Greek architecture, but it could not accommodate the use of arch and vault which characterised Roman architecture.

Some architects, however, took a more pragmatic line. If they could choose between Greek and Roman, why should they not make use of other styles as well? Egyptian, Chinese, Moorish, and Indian influence can be found in the buildings of the late 18th and early 19th centuries, and the Italian Renaissance became increasingly important later. (The brief for the new Royal Exchange in 1839 said that it should be a stone building in 'Grecian, Roman or Italian styles'.) However, the greatest challenge to the Classical styles came from the revival of Gothic, which was seen as specifically Christian in character. The Victorian age, therefore, shows a great variety of historical styles, and many architects were quite prepared to pick and choose, varying their style to suit the type of building they were designing or the preference of their client. C.R. Cockerell's Ashmolean Museum in Oxford (1840) is a successful combination of Greek, Roman and Renaissance elements. Sir Charles Barry, who built the Houses of Parliament in a curiously Classical form of Gothic, also designed in the Renaissance, Greek and Elizabethan styles. Sir George Gilbert Scott worked mainly in the Gothic style and when he was selected in 1862 as architect for the new Foreign Office in Whitehall he submitted a Gothic design; when this was rejected, he offered an alternative in a form of Byzantine; only when this too had been thrown out did he produce the Renaissance version which now stands. The list could be extended but the examples above show how architectural style in the 19th century came to be regarded as little more than a matter of fashion.

The 19th century also saw the most significant advance in the range of building materials since the development of concrete by the Romans. First iron and steel, then reinforced concrete offered new possibilities to the architect. In 1906 the American architects McKim, Mead and White produced a version of the frigidarium from the Baths of Caracalla for the concourse of the Pennsylvania Railroad Station in New York. It was on a scale even larger than the original and was built on a steel frame, clad externally in travertine stone specially imported from near Rome.

It was just this preoccupation with the surface appearance of architecture that was the main target for criticism by the pioneers of the Modern Movement. In 1892, for instance, the American architect Louis Sullivan wrote:

...it would be greatly for our aesthetic good if we could refrain
entirely from the use of ornament for a period of years, in order
that our thought might concentrate acutely upon the production
of buildings well formed and comely in the nude;

and in Holland in 1908, H.P. Berlage claimed that the architect should
concentrate on the creation of spaces rather than the design of facades.

Linked to this distrust of mere ornament was a general belief that
a building's function should be the most important factor in its design,
and other characteristics of the Modern Movement included a willing
acceptance of the technological advances of the 19th and 20th centuries
and a preference for modern materials (e.g. concrete, glass, metal) over
traditional ones (wood, stone, brick). The use of load-bearing walls of
brick or masonry construction was virtually abandoned for large buildings and the system of hanging wall panels from a concrete or metal
frame took its place. Despite these overall similarities, the Modern
Movement was not uniform. Some of the buildings most influential in
its development show what can certainly be described as Classical
influence. Behren's 1908 turbine factory in Berlin (fig. 6.8) is uncom-
promisingly modern in function and materials but in general shape and
in the use of a 'colonnade' of vertical supports down either side it recalls
the Classical temple.

Fig. 6.8 Berlin, AEG Turbine Factory

However, what most people have in mind when they think about 20th century architecture are the concrete or glass slabs which have become so common in our cities, and these have never enjoyed much popular support. One form of reaction against them – it is part of a general Post-Modernist movement which started around 1970 – is to be found in the work of architects who have deliberately turned away from the Modern Movement to build in an explicitly Classical style. In some cases this is just a matter of applying Classical details to an otherwise fairly orthodox modern building, but in others it is more thorough-going. These architects have been drawn back to the 'Classical language of architecture' because they believe that it leads to buildings which possess a natural harmony and can be appreciated on a human scale. Quinlan Terry's Merks Hall (fig. 6.9), built in 1982, illustrates this claim.

It is impossible to predict how this particular Classical revival will develop. What can be asserted with some confidence is that the buildings of ancient Rome, or of any other age before our own, are no more trapped in the past than the great works of literature or music. Their influence will continue and their merits will continue to be reassessed, for dialogue with the past is one of the most powerful means by which we establish our sense of the present and our hopes for the future.

Fig. 6.9 Great Dunmow, Merks Hall

Appendix
Structures and Materials

(a) Structures

The Post and Lintel System

The simplest structural principle which the Romans used in their buildings was the post and lintel system, in which vertical posts support horizontal beams or lintels. The Greeks had employed this to great effect, particularly in their temple architecture: the various types of column – Doric, Ionic, Corinthian – formed the verticals and each had its appropriate horizontal entablature. Influenced by this success, the Romans came to regard the post and lintel system and the use of the orders as the obvious choice for their own temples and for many of their other public buildings.

Its main advantage is its simplicity. Its disadvantage is that the weight of the lintel and of anything resting upon it falls vertically downward (fig. A.1). Only the strength of the lintel itself prevents collapse, and as the posts are moved further apart the risk of this increases. There is, therefore, a limit to the span that can be bridged on this system.

Vitruvius dealt with this problem in one of the chapters he wrote about temples (3.3). He pointed out that if the columns at the front of a

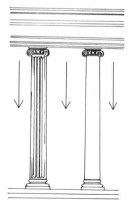
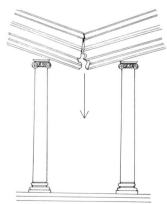

Fig. A.1 Post & lintel

temple were set closely together, the statue in the cella would receive very little light and that women visiting the temple would not be able to enter it arm-in-arm but would have to form single file. The Maison Carrée falls into this category. On the other hand, there were dangers in setting the columns too far apart. Once the gap between adjacent columns equalled the thickness of three columns a stone entablature might break, and if the gap became even wider, the beams had to be made of wood, not stone. This was the case at the Capitolium in Cosa, where the central intercolumniation of the porch was seven times the thickness of the columns.

Arches, Vaults, Domes

The use of the arch avoids this disadvantage and permits the uncluttered roofing of much larger spaces. This is because its shape diverts the downward thrust round the arch itself and then down the vertical supports (fig. A.2 A). At least, that is the theory; in practice, the thrust does not end by moving downward in a perfect vertical but always retains some sideways movement (fig. A.2 B). Hence, the need for arches to be buttressed (figs. 2.1 and 4.10).

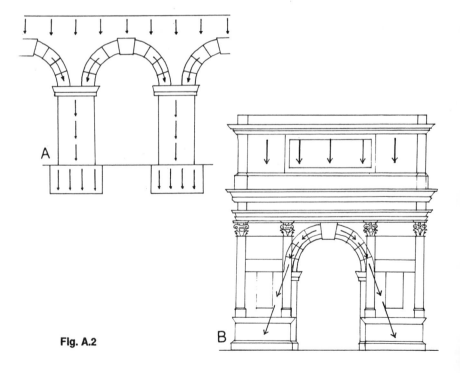

Fig. A.2

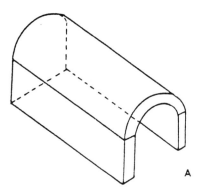 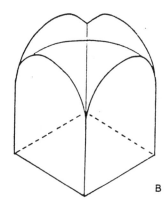

Fig. A.3 Barrel vault & cross vault

Vaults and domes are developments from the basic arch and share its advantages. If the depth of an arch is extended, so that it roofs a space rather than merely marking an entrance, it produces a barrel vault (fig. A.3 A). The apodyterium, tepidarium and caldarium of the Stabian Baths at Pompeii (fig. 4.14) are all roofed with barrel vaults. If two barrel vaults cross at right angles, a cross vault is created (fig. A.3 B); here the weight of the vault is carried only by the four corner points of each bay, and the sides of the bay can be opened up for doors or windows. The Basilica Nova (fig. 4.6) and the frigidarium of the Baths of Caracalla (fig. 4.15) provide good examples. A dome can be described as an arch rotated about its centre point to form a continuous circular shape; the Pantheon (fig. 1.3) or the caldarium of the Baths of Caracalla illustrate this.

(b) Materials

Vitruvius took a detailed interest in the properties of the materials available to him as an architect. In Book 2 he examined the best type of clay for making bricks; explained how to identify the kind of sand most suitable for use in mortar: it should crackle when rubbed in the hand and if thrown on a white garment and then shaken off, should leave no deposit; and distinguished between the types of stone to be burnt for making lime for use in mortar and in stucco. A lengthy chapter (2.9) was devoted to timber: alder, for example, was useless above ground but ideal if one had to sink foundation piles in swampy ground, oak tended to warp when exposed to moisture, and larch had the great advantage of being virtually fireproof.

Stone

Another chapter (2.7) deals with the different kinds of stone which the Roman architects could use. Vitruvius mentions several types of stone available close to Rome. Tufa, formed from solidified volcanic mud, ash and pumice, is easily quarried and durable under cover but crumbles if exposed to the weather, particularly frost. Certain limestones, such as those quarried around Alba Longa or near Gabii, were known to be fire-resistant; the use of stone from Gabii in the Forum of Augustus and in the reconstruction of Rome after the fire of AD 64 has already been mentioned. Another limestone Vitruvius discusses is travertine, found about 20km. east of Rome, which has a creamy and lightly pitted surface appearance. This too is relatively easy to quarry and to cut when first quarried, but hardens on exposure to the air; it stands up well to heavy loads but splits easily in fire. The care exercised by architects in choosing the most appropriate stone for different purposes can be seen in the Colosseum (fig. 4.11): the load-bearing piers are made of travertine – it has been calculated that some 200,000 tonnes were required – while tufa is used only for the load-free walls between them.

Marble

Marble began to come into common use during the reign of Augustus. This explains why Vitruvius, writing early in the reign, hardly refers to it, while Augustus himself could claim towards the end of his reign that he had turned Rome from a city of brick into one of marble. The most important source in Italy itself was the quarries at Carrara. These were in production by 48 BC and produced a close-grained white marble which soon became very popular. Its use in the Macellum at Pompeii is a telling illustration of this, since Pompeii is not a major city and the cost of quarrying and transport would have been considerable. Less surprisingly, it was also used in the Forum of Augustus.

So too were coloured marbles from Africa, Turkey and Greece, an early example of a trend that was to become increasingly popular during the Empire. Coloured marbles, granites and other stones that could be polished to a high sheen were imported from all round the Mediterranean. Some, like the deep maroon porphyry from near the Red Sea, were of a single colour; others, like the violet and white pavonazetto from Turkey, were attractively mottled. The range of colours available also included yellows, greens, grey, and several shades of red. The impact of this use of colour on someone visiting a Roman building can still be appreciated in the Pantheon. In most other cases, however, all that remains is the shell of the building or the bare walls. Fragments of mosaic or marble-patterned floors sometimes remain, but the white or coloured columns and wall panels, the gleam of bronze window grilles and candelabra have gone and can be reconstructed only in our imagination.

Concrete

Concrete probably orginated as a cheaper alternative for stone. An early form was used at Pompeii in the 4th century BC, when house walls were often composed of a framework of local limestone with a core of rubble inside the framework. At first the rubble was held together by clay, but in the following century a proper mortar of lime and sand was developed and this greatly increased the strength of the total mass.

The three essential elements of Roman concrete (facing, core material or aggregate, mortar) are already apparent in this early form. In constructing walls the Romans used to start by building up the facing to a certain height, then put in the core material to the same point, and finally added the mortar. The processs was then repeated until the wall reached its intended height. The facing was obviously important during the construction period and while the mortar was setting, but once it had set hard it was the combination of core material and mortar which provided the real strength of the wall. The much more complex process necessary to construct a concrete vault has already been described in the account of the Pantheon.

Facing styles (fig. A.4) changed over time. In *opus incertum*, the facing consisted of small stones, irregularly set; towards the end of the 2nd century BC this was giving way to *opus reticulatum*, in which the stone facing formed a diagonal pattern rather like a net; the use of horizontal rows of baked brick to provide the facing, *opus testaceum*, may have started around 50 BC but did not replace *opus reticulatum* as the standard form of facing until the reign of Nero.

In walls, the aggregate usually consisted of rubble (smallish lumps of stone – whatever was available locally), but Roman architects became very aware of the need to suit the core material to its position and function in the building. This is very clear in the Pantheon (fig. 1.5): in the foundation ring, the core consists of a rubble of heavy stones, such as travertine; higher up, lighter material is used, until in the dome itself the core material is pumice.

A basic mortar is made of lime and sand with the addition of water, and if correctly mixed this develops strong cohesive qualities once the moisture has evaporated. Mortar like this was used with an aggregate of

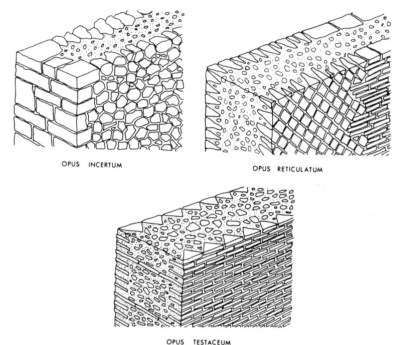

OPUS INCERTUM

OPUS RETICULATUM

OPUS TESTACEUM

Fig. A.4 Styles of brick facing

limestone lumps for the upper part of the city walls at Cosa in the years immediately after its foundation in 273 BC. By the time of Augustus, however, the Romans had realised that they could make an even more effective mortar if they used pozzolana, a volcanic dust, instead of sand. The advantage of this was that it did not need to evaporate out the moisture before becoming cohesive; indeed, as Vitruvius pointed out (2.6.1), it set hard even under water, and so was ideal for harbour works and similar constructions. It was used, for instance, at Ostia in the harbours built by Claudius and Trajan.

One of the earliest major concrete buildings in Rome was the Porticus Aemilia (fig. A.5), an enormous warehouse built beside the Tiber, probably in 193 BC. It is 467m. long and 60m. deep, and consists of a series of barrel vaults set side by side and stepped up from front to back. The chief purpose of this was to accommodate the rise in the level of the land as it ran back from the river, but it also allowed the architect to light the interior by clerestory windows. In this respect and in the way the interior is opened up to provide a large uncluttered space for the transfer and storage of goods, it is an impressive example of Roman functionalism.

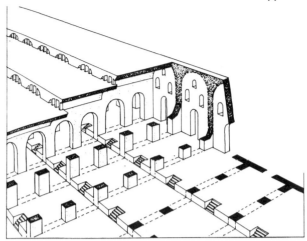

Fig. A.5 Rome, Porticus Aemilia

Yet despite this achievement and the increasingly successful use of concrete in many types of building, Vitruvius took a very cautious line in discussing it. He accepted its value for foundations (3.4.1) and in high-rise tenements (2.8.16) but in general showed a conservative preference for cut stone. That he was not alone in this, and that the feeling against concrete was not easily removed, is demonstrated more than a hundred years later by the choice of travertine for the load-bearing parts of the Colosseum (see above).

(c) The Roman Architectural Revolution

This term refers to the birth of a new and specifically Roman style of architecture, based on a combination of the new structural principle of the arch with the new material, concrete. Concrete has a better strength/weight ratio than stone: for any given space, that is, a concrete vault weighs less than a stone one, and so needs less buttressing; alternatively, a concrete vault can roof a larger space than a stone one of the same weight. It is also more flexible and lends itself to construction in a greater variety of shapes than stone or timber. The combination, therefore, of these two innovations encouraged a new approach to architecture. It freed architects from the constraints under which they and their predecessors had previously laboured and made it possible for them to design from the inside out, starting from the function of the building and the interior shapes that best expressed this. The Pantheon, Basilica Nova, and Baths of Caracalla are all masterpieces of this new style.

Suggestions for Further Study

1. A central skill in the study of architecture is the ability to look at a plan or elevation or at a photograph of a ruined building and visualise the building when complete and in use. Practise this by looking at the plan etc. of a building in your own town and describing what you can see; check your findings by a visit to the actual building. Select the plan of a Roman building (e.g. the Baths of Caracalla) or an area of a Roman city (e.g. the Forum at Pompeii as approached from the Porta Marina) and imagine yourself walking through it. What do you see? What do you feel? What is it about the architecture that creates these feelings?

2. *The building of cities is one of man's greatest achievements. The form of his city always has been and always will be a pitiless indicator of the state of his civilization* (Edmund N. Bacon). How well do Roman cities stand up to examination if judged on this criterion? What about the large cities of present day Britain?

3. Read Vitruvius on the design of cities and their public buildings (1.4-7 & 5.1-12). How many of the issues he considers important are still so regarded by modern architects and town planners? What would Vitruvius think of our 'new towns' (e.g. Milton Keynes, Telford)?

4. Roman towns were taken in at a walking pace. Modern towns should also make visual sense as one drives through them. How has this influenced town planners? Can a town plan work equally well at both speeds?

5. Compare the town you live in with Pompeii or Ostia. Analyse the similarities and differences with regard to the architectural provision for industry, commerce, education, religion, entertainment, residence etc. What does the comparison tell you about the differing priorities of life in ancient Rome and modern Britain?

6. How far do the differences between Greek and Roman architecture and town planning reflect more general differences between the two civilisations?

7. Study the building history of a city in Roman Britain (e.g. London, St. Albans, Wroxeter). What range of public buildings did it have in its period of greatest prosperity? How did this range compare with what one would expect to find in a city in Italy or the south of France at the same time? How similar were the buildings themselves in scale,

design, materials and general appearance?

8. Were there any recognisable differences of architectural style between the different parts of the Roman Empire?

9. The Romans developed a number of successful building-types (e.g. basilica, triumphal arch, baths, dome). Trace the development of one of these (a) through the Roman period, (b) through subsequent ages.

10. Compare the *domus* with a modern detached house or the *insula* with a block of flats. What can you learn from the comparison about the different priorities of life in 1st century AD Pompeii or 2nd century Ostia and 20th century Britain?

11. *A house is a machine for living in* (Le Corbusier). Consider the design and decoration of the *domus* and *insula*. For what kind of life did they prove efficient machines?

12. Should the external appearance of a building express its function? (Always? Slaughter-house? Public Lavatory?) The practice of adding a pedimented entrance porch in Classical style to a steel and concrete super-store has sometimes been criticised as dishonest. Do you agree? Is it any worse than adding engaged columns to the exterior of the Colosseum?

13. Examine the buildings in your own town which are in a Classical style and place them in categories according to the type of use for which they were designed (e.g. educational, residential, commercial). When were they built? Why do you think the architect felt that the Classical style was appropriate? Are there any types of building for which a Classical style is inherently unsuitable?

14. A German philosopher described architecture as *frozen music*. What do you think he meant? Could the phrase help you to appreciate Roman architecture? Would it be equally useful if you were considering the architecture of the Modern Movement?

15. *The most unavoidable of the arts.* How far does the architecture of your home, school/college or town make a positive contribution to your sense of well-being? Or doesn't it?

Suggestions for Further Reading

(1) Vitruvius, *The Ten Books on Architecture,* translated M.H. Morgan, (New York, 1960). Nearly all books on Roman architecture mention Vitruvius but there is no easily available summary of his work and ideas. Useful sections on Roman architects and the architectural profession can be found in (6) and (11a).

(2) R. Brilliant, *Roman Art from the Republic to Constantine* (London, 1974).

(3) Martin Henig (ed.), *A Handbook of Roman Art* (Oxford, 1983).

(4) John Boardman (ed.), *The Oxford History of Classical Art* (Oxford, 1993).

(5) Mortimer Wheeler, *Roman Art and Architecture* (London, 1964).

These general books all contain sections on architecture – in (5) it is the main focus – and on allied arts such as mosaic, stucco and wall painting.

(6) Frank Sear, *Roman Architecture* (London, 1982).

(7) Axel Boethius, *Etruscan & Early Roman Architecture* (Harmondsworth, 1978).

(8) J.B. Ward-Perkins, *Roman Imperial Architecture* (Harmondsworth, 1981).

(9) J.B. Ward-Perkins, *Roman Architecture* (London, 1979).

(10) Frank E. Brown, *Roman Architecture* (London, 1968).

(6) is a well-organised survey of the topic as a whole, with useful sections on techniques and materials and a chapter on Pompeii and Ostia. (7) & (8) were originally published as a single volume in the Pelican History of Art series under the title *Etruscan and Roman Architecture* (1970) and form the standard general treatment of the subject in English; they carry full bibliographies up to the date of publication. (9) contains superb photographs from all parts of the Roman Empire. (10) is a brief introduction, firmly based on the thesis that Roman architecture was the 'art of shaping space around ritual'.

(11) William A. Macdonald, *The Architecture of the Roman Empire*,
  a. Vol. I, *An Introductory Study* (rev. ed., London, 1982)
  b. Vol. II, *An Urban Appraisal* (New Haven, 1986).
(12) I.M. Barton (ed.), *Roman Public Buildings* (Exeter, 1989).
(13) John R. Clarke, *The Houses of Roman Italy* (Oxford, 1991).
(14) M. Lyttleton, *Baroque Architecture in Classical Antiquity* (London, 1974).

Despite its general title, (11) consists of a series of more specialised studies: (11a) contains chapters on the palaces of Nero and Domitian, Trajan's Markets, the Pantheon, architects, techniques and materials. (12) gives a clear summary of its subject, with chapters on town planning, on the different types of building to be found in a Roman city, and on aqueducts. The approach of (13) is apparent from its sub-title, 'Ritual, Space & Decoration'; its argument is built on careful consideration of particular examples from Pompeii, Herculaneum and Ostia, and it is lavishly illustrated. (14) concentrates on the architecture of the eastern parts of the Roman Empire in the light of the tendencies it shares with Italian Baroque.

(15) J.B. Ward-Perkins, *Cities of Ancient Greece and Italy* (London, 1974).
(16) Richard Tomlinson, *From Mycenae to Constantinople* (London, 1992).
(17) David Macaulay, *City* (London, 1975).
(18) T.W. Potter, *Roman Italy* (London, 1987).
(19) S.J. Keay, *Roman Spain* (London, 1988).
(20) Anthony King, *Roman Gaul & Germany* (London, 1990).
(21) H.H. Scullard, *Roman Britain, Outpost of Empire* (London, 1979).
(22) Edmund N. Bacon, *Design of Cities* (London, 1978).

(15) is a clear and succinct description of the main lines of urban development, the argument well supported by plans and photographs. It should be supplemented by (11b), a rich and stimulating account of the elements of urban architecture and the way they contribute to the total effect of the Roman city. (16) contains useful chapters on the building history of Rome, Pompeii, Leptis Magna and Palmyra. (17), described when it first appeared as 'for children of all ages', shows the foundation and development of a Roman city in the Po valley by means of a series

of excellent drawings. (18) is an admirably clear general survey, combining different types of evidence effectively and maintaining a good balance between general themes and particular examples; like its companion volumes, (19) & (20), it contains material on urban development and architecture. (21) provides similar evidence for Britain. Of the books listed above, (6), (8), (9), (11b) also deal with the architecture of the provinces. (22) covers a range of cities from Athens to Philadelphia and Peking to Brasilia; there is little directly on the Roman city but its combination of text, plans, diagrams, engravings and photographs is brilliantly successful in suggesting ways of seeing and assessing urban development.

(23) Donald R. Dudley, *Urbs Roma* (London, 1967).

(24) William L. Macdonald, *The Pantheon* (Cambridge, Mass, 1976).

(25) Susan Walker & Andrew Burnett, *The Image of Augustus* (London, 1981).

Urbs Roma (23) is a source book of texts on the building history of Rome and on the individual monuments, well illustrated. (24) offers a clear account of the design, meaning and influence of the Pantheon. [Two recent articles on this building are also worth attention: Paul Davies, David Hemsoll, & Mark Wilson Jones, 'The Pantheon: Triumph of Rome or Triumph of Compromise?, *Art History*, Vol. 10, No 2 (June 1987); Paul Godfrey & David Hemsoll, 'The Pantheon: temple or rotunda? in Martin Henig & Anthony King (eds), *Pagan Gods & Shrines in the Roman Empire* (Oxford University Committee for Archaeology, 1986).] (25), written to accompany a British Museum exhibition, contains useful material on the Forum of Augustus, his Mausoleum, and the Ara Pacis.

(26) R. Meiggs, *Roman Ostia* (2nd edn, Oxford, 1973).

(27) Gustav Hermansen, *Ostia* (Edmonton, Alberta, 1982).

(28) Peter Connolly, *Pompeii* (Oxford, 1990).

(29) Marcel Brion, *Pompeii & Herculaneum* (London, 1960).

(30) Michael Grant, *Cities of Vesuvius* (London, 1971).

(31) J.B. Ward-Perkins and Amanda Claridge, *Pompeii, AD 79* (Bristol, 1976).

(32) L. Richardson Jr, *Pompeii, an Architectural History* (Baltimore, 1988).

(33) Roger Ling, 'A New Look at Pompeii', in Barry Cunliffe (ed.), *Origins* (London, 1987).

(34) Andrew Wallace-Hadrill, 'The Social Structure of the Roman House', *PBSR*, 56 (1988).
(35) F.E. Brown, *Cosa, the Making of a Roman Town* (Ann Arbor, 1980).
(36) Iain Browning, *Jerash & The Decapolis* (London, 1982).

Both Ostia & Pompeii are dealt with in general books on Roman architecture; see especially (6) – (10), (13), (16). On Ostia, (26) is a detailed general history, including its public and domestic architecture, and (27) provides useful information on the internal lay-out of the insula. There is no really good book on Pompeii and Herculaneum. Like (17), (28) is aimed at a relatively young readership but its reconstruction drawings convey a considerable amount of information, and (31), originally written as an exhibition guide, contains good introductory essays; (32) is a full and detailed account but suffers from poor illustrations and lack of plans and from its inadequate treatment of the social context of the architecture; the two articles, (33) & (34), both make excellent starting points for studying Pompeii and its housing. For Cosa, (35) provides a lively account of the foundation and early years of a Roman colony. (36), well illustrated by the author's drawings as well as by photographs, provides a good introduction to the architecture and town planning of the eastern part of the Roman Empire; there are also books by Browning on *Palmyra* and *Petra*.

(37) Donald Strong & David Brown (eds), *Roman Crafts* (London, 1976).
(38) K.D. White, *Greek & Roman Technology* (London, 1984).
(39) A.T. Hodge, *Roman Aqueducts & Water Supply* (London, 1989).

Both (37) & (38) contains useful information on the crafts and technology associated with architecture. (39) is now the standard work on its subject.

(40) John Summerson, *The Classical Language of Architecture* (London, 1980).

Written in a clear and lively style and with a good choice of illustrations, this makes an excellent introduction to the after-life of Classical architecture up to its date of publication.

Glossary of Architectural Terms

The explanation of terms not found here may occur in the main text and should be located by consulting the Index.

Apse A semi-circular recess, usually with a roof in the shape of a half-dome.

Capital The top part of a column. Each of the three main **Orders** had its own type of capital.

Capitolium A temple dedicated to the Capitoline Triad (Jupiter, Juno, Minerva), often sited in a position overlooking the main forum of a Roman city as a sign of its pride in being part of the Roman world; the name comes from the Temple of Jupiter built on the Capitol, one of the seven hills of Rome.

Cardo, Decumanus Terms borrowed from the technical vocabulary of surveying to describe the streets that make up the grid in a Roman city; the **cardo** ran north-south, the **decumanus**, east-west.

Corinthian The slenderest of the three main **orders** and the one most commonly used by the Romans (fig. G.1).

Curia In Rome, the Senate House; elsewhere, the meeting place for the local council, often adjacent to the Basilica.

Doric The sturdiest of the three main orders (fig. G.2). Greek Doric had no base, Roman Doric often did.

Engaged Column A column is engaged if it does not stand free but is partly embedded in the wall against which it stands, as on the side and back walls of the Maison Carrée at Nîmes, or around the outside of the Colosseum.

Entablature The horizontal part of an **order**, resting upon the capital of a column and consisting of architrave, frieze and cornice (fig. G.3, the **Corinthian** entablature).

Ionic Usually differed from the Corinthian only in capital (fig. G.4)

Monolith The shaft of a column is usually made up of separate drums; a **monolith** is a column shaft consisting of a single piece of stone. They were usually **unfluted.**

Nymphaeum An elaborately built and decorated fountain, usually having tiers of superimposed columns flanking niches with statues; sometimes used to punctuate the streetscape of a Roman city.

Orders An order consists of a column and its appropriate entablature. Vitruvius (3.5 & 4.1-6) described the three main orders used by the Romans – **Corinthian, Doric, Ionic** – and explained how their design was governed by a series of proportions between their different parts. He also (4.7) described the **Tuscan** order.

Pediment The triangular space between the entablature and the gable roof of a temple or building of similar shape; a decorative architectural feature derived from this, either triangular or segmental.

Peristyle A continuous colonnade; in Roman architecture, usually surrounding an interior space (as in a domus); sometimes also applied to the colonnade running round the outside of a temple.

Pilaster An **engaged pillar.**

Pillar A column of square or rectangular section.

Podium A raised platform forming the base of a temple or other building.

Tholos A round or polygonal building, generally small in scale.

Tuscan A squat version of **Doric**, often thought to convey an impression of primitive strength, **unfluted.**

Unfluted An column is unfluted if it lacks the usual vertical grooving.

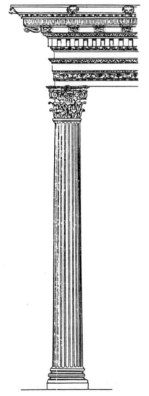 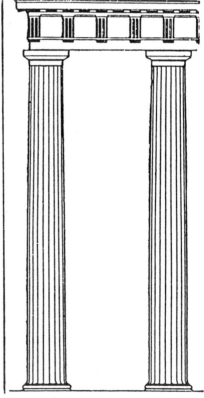

Fig. G.1 Corinthian order
[Courtesy of D. Yarwood, *The Architecture of Europe*, Batsford, London, 1974]

Fig. G.2 Doric Order

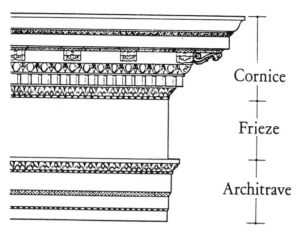

Cornice

Frieze

Architrave

Fig. G.3 Corinthian entablature

Fig. G.4 Ionic Order

THE ROMAN EMPIRE

1. Lancaster
2. York
3. Wroxeter
4. Leicester
5. Caerwent
6. St. Albans
7. London
8. Paris
9. Coblenz
10. Cologne
11. Mainz
12. Bourges
13. Autun
14. Besancon
15. Strasbourg
16. Augst
17. Lyons
18. Orange
19. Nimes
20. Arles
21. Marseilles
22. Narbonne
23. Saragossa
24. Barcelona
25. Valencia
26. Timgad
27. Dugga
28. Carthage
29. Leptis Magna
30. Athens
31. Alexandria
32. Jerash
33. Palmyra
34. Constantinople

107

ITALY

1. Aosta
2. Como
3. Pavia
4. Piacenza
5. Brescia
6. Mantua
7. Verona
8. Vicenza
9. Venice
10. Spina
11. Bologna
12. Carrara
13. Arrezo
14. Fano
15. Cosa

16. Rome
17. Gabii
18. Ostia
19. Alba Longa
20. Naples
21. Herculaneum
22. Pompeii
23. Poseidonia/Paestum

Index